From Welfare

to

Faring Well

Journey to Success

Sherman L. Whitfield

ISBN: 978-1-7352672-1-0
LCCN: 2019920347
Published by Maximized Productions, LLC.
UPH Publishing Div.
6715 Suitland Rd. – Morningside, MD 20746
www.maximizedproductions.com
Cover Design: Maximized Productions, LLC.
UPH Pub. Div.
Book Design by Dawn M. Harvey

Please direct your inquiries to the address above or visit:
www.whitfieldmotivations.com or
www.maximizedproductions.com

PRINTED IN THE UNITED STATES OF AMERICA

Philippians 4:13

"I can do all things through Christ who strengthens me."

DEDICATION

I dedicate this work to my Mother. Lucy Dale Whitfield has gone through a lot in her life, and she is 92 years old at the time of this book's publication. We affectionately call her "Mother Dear." She is a two-time cancer survivor and has had to overcome many trials and tribulations in her life. But she never gives up or complains.

She has been a Mother of the Church of God in Christ for over thirty years and is the recipient of many plaques and awards for her church work. My mother has a list of eighteen church members that she calls daily, in addition to her family, just to check to see how they are doing. She calls it her mission work. She raised six children and has never had to go to the jailhouse to visit any of us or had to get us out of legal troubles. She counts this as one of her major achievements.

Mother Dear's philosophy on life can best be surmised by reflecting on her recitation at numerous family gatherings of a toast which provides as follows:

"We have long to live and much to do. Let our good behavior carry us through. Peace at home and pleasure abroad; treat your friends right and serve the good Lord.

In summer time, we raise watermelon. In winter time, we raise pumpkin. Christmas comes but once a year, and everybody's looking for something!

But, when you're dead in your grave, your bones bleached white as cotton; the good times we've had together today will never be forgotten!

I also dedicate this work to my father. While he was absent for large parts of my life, I recognize that without him I wouldn't exist. My father fought in World War II. He never went into detail about the time he spent in the war. Indeed, it wasn't until his death that the family found his discharge papers revealing he had received the Bronze Star and three Bronze Service Stars, as well as many other honors for valiance for his military service.

PFC Benjamin Whitfield, Sr. loyally served his country as an enlisted infantryman in the United States Army from May 26, 1942 through November 20, 1945. He fought for our country, but when he returned home he was denied the rights afforded white veterans. I've often wondered who he would have been, who I might be, indeed, who many African American's might be, had our country been more humane or if they would have just been reasonable. If, after seeing how African Americans fought and died alongside white-Americans in the war, they had allowed us to prosper. If they had afforded us the same benefits given our fellow white Americans, benefits like the GI Bill which allowed white veterans to obtain loans for housing, provided rights to employment and rights to educational benefits. If that had happened, where would we be today? Only God knows. But, my Father served his country only to return home to be treated as less than a man. Understanding that truth, I give him credit for what he did achieve in his life and forgive him for the neglect we experienced and the abandonment we felt growing up.

ACKNOWLEDGEMENTS

Jesus Christ deserves the credit for my life, all of it. That is the truth. Period. Without Him, there would be no Sherman and no story to tell.

To my wife, Paula—the love of my life, my true and best friend. Thank you for all of your love and support. You saw in me what I never saw in myself. You were my editor, advisor, memory jogger, and the inspirer for this book. It is your faith in me and your unceasing support that propels me onward and upward. For that, and so much more, I will always love, honor and cherish you with my whole heart.

To my brother, Benjamin, Jr., you are my oldest friend and confidant. Thank you for your leadership, your love and your unrelenting faith in me. I love you my brother.

To my brother Larry, who like our Father served our country in the Army and was the first of my siblings to travel outside of the United States to Korea where you served, I learned so much from the experiences you shared with me. You planted in me a curiosity that made me open to embrace diversity in other people and other cultures. Those are qualities that have benefited me immensely throughout my journey. I love you my brother.

To my oldest sister Sender Reatha, your cooking skills as a young girl provided us with simple but delicious meals. They fueled our bodies and warmed our spirits. Indeed, they provide some of my fondest memories to this very day. I love you my sister.

To my second sister Naomi, your courageous no-nonsense disposition has always inspired pride. You were one of the first of us to step out on your own and have always maintained a strong spirit of independence. I'm proud of you, and I love you my sister.

And, to my youngest sister Levette, you've given both joy and laughter to us all since the day you were born. Your attentive care for our mother is ever-present, and you are a wonderful mother to your three sons. I love you my baby sister.

To my Uncle Hules and Aunt Ola Dale, you both played immensely important roles in my life growing up.   Uncle, you were a father figure, mentor, and teacher. You taught me what it meant to be a man of responsibility and integrity. Auntie, you shared your home with my brothers and I. And you treated us with love and kindness, sharing with us when you had very little. Thank you both from the bottom of my heart. I love you.

INTRODUCTION

I finished one of my motivational speeches to students at a university; it was received well. I received applause and admiration from the crowd and, as usual, was asked a question I had been asked many times before: "Do you have a book that tells your story?" My answer was the same as always, "Not yet, but I am working on one."

In truth, I was working on a book but not with any sense of urgency. I had become very successful in life and writing a book was a big deal that required a lot of soul searching. It would require me to reflect upon and deal with memories, some that I would rather forget. With the urging of friends and family, I took on the task to share "the rest of my story." In a thirty to forty-five-minute speech, I was barely scratching the surface of my story. I knew that there was so much more that I could share and, to truly help others, believed I *should* tell.

There have been many books written about moving from rags to riches. What makes mine different? I would say the big difference is that this is "*my*" rags to riches story. Of all the books that have been written on this subject, none of them were *my* story. I believe my story will move and touch the hearts of people in a different way than other books.

This book is not only about overcoming trials and tribulations, but it also seeks to reveal my true heart, my underlying motivation and the character it takes to rise above poverty to enduring riches. Therefore, I am writing to motivate, encourage and give hope to people who feel hopeless. The most important message that I want the reader to hear is that we live in the greatest and most prosperous country on earth. Making daily sound choices affords one the greatest opportunities to rise from poverty to riches in our great land.

I grew up black and poor. I am still black, but I made the decision, with the help of my God, and through his Son, Jesus Christ, not to remain poor. This book will detail my journey to success. It will explain how I overcame many trials and tribulations along the way to become the person that I am today. My ultimate goal is to make a difference in my own life, as well as in the lives of those that I encounter. Growing up, I had no problem accepting help when necessary, but I totally refused to become a victim and accept pity. I didn't want, nor would I accept, an excuse not to be successful. Yet, I found that there are plenty of people willing to give you reasons to fail. Some basic reasons are poverty, a broken home, abuse, lack of education and physical disability. I learned from the great speaker and writer, Jim Rohn, that these are all part of a disease called "excusitis."

This work will be a success if it helps to encourage one person to make a difference with his or her life; and, if it convinces one reader not to give up on themselves — even if society gives up on them. My ultimate goal is to help others to look at *everyday* as one day, one step on their life's journey of success.

A Word About Sherman

Sherman's story could have been entitled "From Rags to Riches," "From Failure to Success" or maybe even "Moving On Up." But none of these over-used titles would have captured the true-life story of Sherman. His life can best be described as a Journey of Success. This is because in every obstacle or temporal failure that he encountered, he not only saw a challenge he could overcome, he saw an opportunity he could turn into success through integrity, discipline and continued growth. He envisioned every day of his life as a successful step forward on his life's journey. Sherman's goal wasn't just to achieve financial wealth or security. His goal was to make the best of his life, make the best of any mistakes, continuously learning from them, and to enjoy the resulting benefits that would naturally flow through. And, yes, while financial security followed, it was but a nonessential consequence that he would accept as he celebrated the true successes of a life dedicated to those principles.

Sherman realized at an early age that these qualities were the true keys to success. He also knew that making the right choice wasn't always going to be easy. But, smart choices *would* provide long-lasting positive results. While perhaps it is easier in the short-term, poor decision-making would produce devastating life-altering results in the end. In other words, doing what is right can be hard to do but easier to live *with*; while making the wrong choices can be easy to do but much harder to live *through*. Sherman looked at each day as a successful day, not waiting for some future time in his life to claim success. Success is a journey, not a destination. He was always successful, not in the way most people today would define it with fame and fortune, but his life was a success just the same. Each day he had options and choices; whether to be guided by the principles he knew would benefit him long term or driven by the quick gain he could achieve by making the wrong choice. He wasn't perfect, far from it. Indeed, his journey continues even to this day. But, each day lived is a day filled with options; the better choices one makes, the more options one will have in life.

What makes Sherman's story so relevant is that his story can be *your* story. You just need to decide today that you will live using the principles of integrity, discipline and continuous learning to make the right choices. This decision will bring you success and options in life that can lead you, not only to financial wealth, but also to wealth of caring, wealth of spirit, wealth of respect and wealth of leadership. Sherman's underlying message is that one shouldn't make financial wealth the goal, instead let financial wealth be the consequence of the successful implementation of the goals achieved. Simply put, don't chase after money, let money chase after and find you.

TABLE OF CONTENTS

CHILDHOOD LIFE...25

FAMILY RELATIONS..37

GROWING UP...42

COTTON CHOPPING AND COTTON PICKING...........54

LESSONS I'VE LEARNED ALONG THE WAY...........66

MY MOTHER THE CIVIL RIGHTS ACTIVIST.............83

ONE STEP AT A TIME..91

CAREER BEGINNINGS~GENERAL MOTORS..........101

DIVORCE..116

NEWLY MARRIED ~ MORE LIFE CHANGES...........131

MY NEW ROLE AT ALLISON ENGINE COMPANY ...155

MOVING TO LONDON..168

RETURNING TO LILLY CORPORATE HEADQUARTERS
....207

How Do I Use My Journal Pages?

It is Sherman's hope that as he shares
his life and lessons with you, that you
too will pen the lessons you learn
while reading this book. Also, feel free
to write your memories, goals and
dreams on your journal pages.

CHAPTER ONE

CHILDHOOD LIFE

The year was 1948, the same year that U.S. President Harry S. Truman signed the Executive Order 9981 ending racial segregation in the United States Armed Forces, and the WAF was created allowing Women in the Air Force. In this same year, a baby was born to a poor black woman whose name was Lucy Whitfield. He was the second child born to Lucy, and her husband was Benjamin F. Whitfield, Sr. This baby's given name was Sherman Lee Whitfield. I was named after William Tecumseh Sherman who served as a General in the Union Army during the American Civil War. My mother did not want to offend her southern roots, so she added the middle name, Lee. This was the name of a Confederate officer, General Robert E. Lee. I sometimes wonder if being named after two virulent men of war was somehow prophetic. My name is emblematic of conflict and of one of the most changing times in American history.

My life's journey began at a time of change for black people and for women in particular. However, it would take another twenty years before any of the changes would have an impact on me, my journey to success, or any true change, was achieved for the black community.

I am the second oldest of six children. I have two brothers, one older and one younger; and three younger sisters. Each of us is a different skin color. When I was young, I was given the nickname "white boy," because I was lighter-skinned and had red hair. This was not a nickname of endearment. Early on, my Dad told me he wasn't my real father. He claimed my real father was a white man by the name of Mr. Polk, the owner of the land that we lived on. My father was a sharecropper on Mr. Polk's land. My mother assured me that Mr. Polk wasn't my father. She explained that my father's grandfather was a white man, and that was where I got my fairer complexion and red hair. My oldest sister had very light skin with freckles and red hair. It was not unusual for my father to question the parentage of his children. He believed in the old saying, "mama's baby, daddy's maybe." I guess that was because my father was credited with having over thirty children by many different women. This may explain his hesitancy in claiming every child that he was told he'd fathered.

I was six years old, barefoot and wearing a hand-me-down t-shirt and short pants. It was a late afternoon at dusk dark. The day was hot, and the family was sitting on the front porch of our two-room house. There was a big tree directly in front of the house that helped shield us from the scorching sun. As the sun faded and the evening darkness crept across the sky, the family would sit on the front porch. The adults would be talking grownup stuff. And a bucket filled with old rags from worn-out clothes was set afire, and then smothered down to produce smoke. The smoke would cause our eyes to water and burn, but also kept the mosquitoes away. The front door was propped open allowing the smoke to enter the house and, hopefully, dissuade the mosquitoes from coming inside. As we sat, we would hear stories of our parents' lives. The conversation was like a fountain, flowing and never-ending. The stories were filled with laughter, joy, and some angst. Our culture was like a revival of sorts. We sang old songs and heard old stories. Things we'd heard many times before but told with an intensity that kept the tales new. We looked at ourselves, and at each other, with a sense of anticipation. There was pride, even reverence for who we were, what we could aspire to, and those we had descended from.

My father would talk about how he never got paid what was due him from sharecropping; that his boss would always say that the crop didn't do as well as expected so he couldn't pay my father what he had promised. My mother didn't work in the cotton fields. She was a self-taught beautician. She would shampoo, press and style the women's hair in the neighborhood. They'd reminisce about how my mother's parents had owned a store in town and had for a time made a relatively good living selling needed goods in the community. My mother's father also was a holiness preacher that had raised his family with a stern hand.

My parents taught us that we should respect older people and how we should behave in general. They especially emphasized that we had to respect all white people and never talk back to them. They drilled into us the need, always, to say "yes sir" and "yes ma'am" to adults, and invariably to white folks.

We would sit there eating pecans, peanuts and brazil nuts. We would throw the shells on the ground for the birds or other creatures to use in nesting. Birds and pigeons would become a source of food for us as time went on. If we were lucky, we had sweet water to drink. This was water with sugar or honey added to it. We didn't have ice to put in the drinks because ice cost money. It was bought by the block from the icehouse in town. But we never complained about not having ice for our sweet water; we were taught never to complain about anything.

At bedtime, around eight o'clock most evenings, my mother would tell us to take a bath. Baths took place in a number three washtub. The tub was round, made of tin and measured about three feet round and three feet high. The tub was also meant to be used for hand-washing clothes with a washboard. We didn't have a washing machine. We would fill the washtub with water from the hand pump on our back porch. We'd prime the pump with water in order to get the water to come up out of the ground. Once we got the water flowing, we would continue to pump it until we had what we needed. Then, we'd heat up a bucket of water on the wood-burning stove and pour it in the tub. We'd have a contest to see who would be the first one in the tub. We were all dirty from playing outside in the yard and on unpaved roads all day, so the water was filthy after the first person took a bath. It got dirtier and colder after each person took their turn. We also played a game to see who could hold their head under the water in the bathtub the longest. We didn't have a television, so we made up games to entertain ourselves.

Our bed was made of iron. A cotton mattress rested atop wood slats. The cotton mattress made the bed very hot in the summer; we'd sweat all night. As we got settled into bed, my mother would spread the cover over us and tell a bedtime story.

At the tender age of seven, my older brother Ben took on the responsibility of storytelling. He had already begun to show maturity well beyond his age. As soon as the oil lamp was blown out, Ben would start to tell a story. He created his own characters, both heroes and villains. His favorite bedtime stories always involved cowboys. The cowboys would come to town and start trouble, and the hero would come to the rescue. The rest of us would ask him questions about the hero; our questions were based on how we wanted the hero to behave. My brother Ben would always answer, "Yes that is what is going to happen." So, he actually allowed us to help him construct the story. We would listen intently until we fell asleep.

Within thirty minutes, unwanted guests would start to invade our attempts to sleep. The first uninvited guests were the mosquitoes. They would buzz before they would bite; the buzzing was more annoying than the bite. We wanted them to land so that we could kill them. Often they would sing and land, then they'd bite and suck blood from our bodies. We'd swat them with our hands to kill them or to make them go away. This battle with the mosquitoes would continue off and on all night. My mother would get out of the bed and spray the room with Black Flag. This was a very potent solution of chemicals that would be illegal today to use around humans. We welcomed it and would cover our heads as our mother sprayed the room. This would stop the invasion for a while, but then it was like the pests would regroup and the singing and biting would start again.

The next sleep disrupters would start their attacks later in the night. These bloodsuckers were more fierce than the mosquitoes. These were the chinches, also known as bed bugs. "Goodnight, sleep tight; don't let the bed bugs bite." This little bed-time rhyme may not be recognized by today's youngsters. Yet, in rural areas in the mid-forties and fifties, it truly described the situation. What are chinches? Perhaps we had the name wrong. The encyclopedia describes chinches as a garden pest and refers to the bed pest as bed bugs. In any event, my mother referred to the annoying pests that inhabited the mattress as chinches.

Webster's Dictionary says that chinches, or bed bugs, are small wingless insects that feed on blood. They live in mattresses and bite their vulnerable victims while they sleep piercing the skin with their sharp beaks. The creatures are reddish-brown and when mature are about a quarter of an inch long. Because of its small size, it can hide in crevices or small folds in a mattress, bed quilts or sheets. They sleep during the day and hunt for food during the night. Their bites are very annoying and cause the skin to swell and itch.

We felt helpless against these invaders because they seemed to enjoy the insecticides. They acted as if it was their favorite cocktail. We had to squeeze them between our fingers to kill them. As we did this, our blood came out onto the sheets. They would hide and sleep in the cotton mattress during the day and come out at night to eat; our bodies provided the feast. I longed for morning, because the chinches hid during the day. Daylight revealed the blood-stained sheets and dead chinches, providing visual evidence of the nightly battle between the species.

This battle went on for about four years until my mother was able to buy an innerspring mattress which seemed to slow down the chinch infestation. Seemingly, the innerspring mattress didn't provide them as much comfort or as sufficient a hiding place.

The battle with the mosquitoes and chinches was a time in my life that I felt most helpless. I felt that I was fighting with an enemy trying to survive on my blood, and they never gave up. In reality, I learned a life lesson from one of the most difficult times in my young life that would pay dividends as I got older. The lesson, never give up.

At an early age, these experiences taught me a lot about life. I learned that some of the happiest times in my life were the simplest times. There were good times like sitting on the porch and eating pecans with my parents, waiting in expectation for the action-packed bedtime stories imagined by my older brother, and the affection and laughter of my siblings as we drifted to sleep. My imagination would be in full gear as I listened to Ben's action-filled tales. Yet, we also dealt nightly with the battle of the mosquitoes and chinches. But, we endured, and we survived.

Five of us slept in one standard-sized bed until my older sister, Sender Reatha, reached the age of seven. My younger sister, Naomi, was four. My brother, Ben, was twelve; I was ten and my brother, Larry, was nine years old. My brothers and I slept at the head of the bed, and my sisters slept at the foot. In the summer, this sleeping arrangement was very uncomfortable. It was hot, and we didn't have air conditioning. Sweat ran down our backs like a river. Occasionally, when the night was especially sweltering, one or two of us would lie on the floor which was a little cooler. And, sleeping on the floor eliminated the issue of chinches. Once Sender Reatha turned seven, my mother bought a wood-framed standard-sized bed from the second-hand store. That's where we purchased all of our furniture and any other durable household items. My sisters finally had their own bed to sleep in. This was a great benefit, because it provided more space for all of us.

We all were ecstatic. My two sisters, Sender Reatha and Naomi, no longer had to share the bed with us. They slept in the new bed, and we three boys slept in the other. Up to that point, our youngest sister Levette had slept with Mother Dear. Once the new bed was acquired, Levette was delighted to hop into the girls' bed with her two older sisters.

The boys' bed was a standard-sized iron bed. As we got older and bigger, it became very uncomfortable for the three boys to sleep in the same bed. Yet, there was no other option. To deal with the situation, we slept in "the spoon" position. This meant that we all slept facing the same direction. When one of us turned over during the night, all of us had to turn or the person on the end would fall out of the bed. These close sleeping arrangements were beneficial in the winter months, because our bodies helped to keep us warm from the cold wind blowing through the cracks in the walls. In the summer months, however, the sleeping arrangement was hot and uncomfortable. One advantage was that it served as cover when one of us wet the bed. This happened quite often in the winter months when no one wanted to get up from a warm bed into the freezing temperatures to use the slop-jar to relieve themselves. It should be noted, we were all well past the age when we may have reasonably been urinating in the bed. The youngest would be blamed for the mishap, even if they weren't the guilty party.

House

Life was simple. Even though we didn't have electricity or indoor plumbing in the house, it was no big deal because our neighbors didn't have electricity or indoor plumbing either. We didn't get electrical wiring in the house until I was six years old. Before that, we used oil lamps for lighting in the rooms. Indoor plumbing wasn't installed until I reached the age of twelve. Before then, a slop-jar was used to handle eliminated waste. The slop-jar was a tin container covered in white porcelain. We placed it beside the bed to use at night, and we'd get up in the morning and empty the slop-jar into the outdoor toilet. The outdoor toilet was about twenty feet from the house and was equipped with the Sears and Roebuck catalog which served as toilet paper. The outdoor toilet was made of unfinished wood; the seat was a wooden board with a hole in it set over a hole in the ground. You sat there to relieve yourself. The foundation also was made of wood and was very unstable. A strong wind would occasionally blow it over. There was no mechanism available to get rid of the waste; therefore, the location was a constant draw for flies and there were thousands upon thousands of maggots swimming in the place during the summer months. The odor from the outdoor toilet could reach the house depending on the direction that the wind blew. In the summer months, the heat from the tin roof helped create an oven-like atmosphere inside the house. We had a small electric fan we'd use to cool the house down and also deal with some of the periodic abhorrent smells.

On Halloween night, boys would go through the neighborhood and push over the neighbors' toilets. It was our way of having fun. The next morning, there wasn't much of a mystery who the responsible parties were. We'd be scolded and told to go and set the toilets back in place.

We lived in a two-room, wood-framed house with a tin roof. This style of house was called a shotgun house because you could shoot a shotgun through the front door, and the bullet could go out of the back door without hitting anything in the house. Of course, that was also because there wasn't much furniture in the house to hit. I could have been a weatherman. Before I got out of bed in the morning, I knew the forecast. There was no drywall to provide added insulation, so the decaying wood, along with the holes in the tin roof facilitated our weather reporting ability. Whether it was rain, sleet, snow, cold or heat we knew it. If it was raining outside, it would rain on us inside as we slept. If it snowed, which thankfully was rare in Arkansas, the snow would find every crack or crevasse in the wall of the house and come inside. During those times, the house felt like a refrigerator. It was normal to have little piles of snow on the floor where it had come through the cracks in the walls of the house. Without heat, the piles would remain until we made a fire in the wood-burning stove.

We made the best of it; made lemonade out of lemons so to speak. When it snowed we'd gather snow off the floor, add powdered milk and sugar to make ice cream. We had a wood-burning pot-belly stove located in the front room to warm our two-room home. Our bedroom was located in the back of the house, so it wasn't as warm. The pot-belly stove was made of tin. When the fire turned the stove red hot, my siblings and I would stand around the stove to keep warm.

We usually cooked on top of the stove. But we'd put sweet potatoes inside the stove atop the fire to cook them. It was not uncommon for us to get burned, either as a result of standing too close to the stove or from retrieving the sweet potatoes from the hot ashes inside.

When I was ten, my mother didn't have the money to buy wood for our wood-burning stove. It was expensive to burn wood if you were poor. We used this stove for both cooking and heating the house. There was an old house next to ours that had belonged to my grandmother. No one had lived in it for years. Therefore, we used it to fuel our wood-burning stove. It became our utility source during the winter. We basically took the house down, board by board, cutting the wood into pieces to fit into our stove. This allowed us to cook food and to keep warm for the winter.

Medicine

Living in these conditions made us easy victims for colds and other childhood diseases. My mother couldn't afford to take us to the doctor or to buy medicine. Whether we got sick with a cold, caught chicken pocks, measles, or mumps, my mother would resort to a home remedy. Most of the remedies involved alcohol and oil mixed with dried corn shucks. She would take the corn shucks, boil them, pour off the liquid and add some home brewed alcohol that was purchased at the local juke joint. There were no labels on the bottles of alcohol; we called it "white lighting." It was as clear as water but had a punch that would make a person five-feet-tall and weighing a hundred pounds believe they could level Muhammad Ali, the heavyweight champion of the world. Simply put, it had a very high concentration of alcohol.

When we suffered a cut, we'd cover it with dirt from the ground. This would stop the bleeding and help build a scab over the wound. When we got burned from standing too close to the stove, we'd put cooking grease on the spot. Table salt was another cure-all. It could be used for cuts, burns, swellings or any other external injury.

Growing up in these poor conditions served only to make me more determined to succeed in life. I had no idea what field of study or job I wanted. I had but one criterion; the job needed to require that I wear a necktie. In my mind, anyone who wore a tie to work was successful. Male schoolteachers were the only people that I saw on a regular basis that wore ties. I didn't have a role model or mentor that I could talk to about what success looked like or what it took to prepare for or to attend college. But there was a drive inside of me to succeed, even before I knew what that was or where it would take me.

My motivation to be successful was to help my mother and family. At no point growing up did I consider that I was going to remain poor. I would tell people that while I would always be black, I would not always be poor.

Journey to Success Notes:

CHAPTER TWO

FAMILY RELATIONS

Growing up, I never saw my parents show affection or love for one another. It may have been there, but it was not on outward display for us to see. My parents argued often; the arguments focused on whatever my Dad was or was not doing. My recollection is that the focus of discord was around him not providing adequate food, clothing, and shelter for the household. He did, however, maintain company and involvement with other women. The sounds of yelling and profuse profanity were common in our home growing up. And, there was physical fighting on occasion. Indeed, we could count on a physical confrontation almost every weekend when both my mother and father would come home intoxicated, having consumed bootleg white lighting.

My mother was taller and heavier than my father. He was five feet nine inches tall and weighed about one hundred fifty pounds. My mother weighed over three hundred pounds and was six feet tall. She'd say that she didn't really know how much she weighed because the scale would only go up to three hundred pounds. She was my father's third wife and was fifteen years younger than him. She said she married my father to get out of her parents' house. My mother and father had a very rocky marriage. The only consolation for us was that when they did have physical confrontations, my mother always won.

Vividly, I remember one weekend when they got into a fight. My mother took the yard rake, hit my father and split his lip. It created a scar that lasted the rest of his life. Another time they got into a fight; my mother struck my father with a tool cracking his forehead open. I can still hear him now, screaming loudly, "Woman, you've busted my skull." The whole experience was frightening, and my siblings and I would run and hide when the fights broke out. My younger siblings would cry and beg my parents to stop fighting. It was a devastating scene; I deplored it and the violence we witnessed. I vowed to never hit or misuse a woman. I have kept that vow.

Father Leaves the Family

My father left us when I was five or six years old to go to Chicago to find work. To be fair, there wasn't much work for a black man in the rural South, other than sharecropping, and that just never worked out for my Dad. He went "up North," as we called it, to find better employment. He did find a job in Chicago at a plant that manufactured cookies. He periodically sent money back home to my mother. His financial support became less frequent as time went by. You see, my father had found someone else and started another family in Chicago. He would come back to Arkansas for visits and would bring his new family with him. He and my mother never got a divorce, but that didn't stop my father from having five more children with the woman that he lived with in Chicago.

My mother never spoke to us negatively about our father. We always loved him. She knew of the challenges that my father and other men of color had to face each day of their lives living in the Jim Crow Era. This meant that my father was treated as less than a man. In every area of his life, he faced discrimination and segregation at water fountains, restaurants, stores, all public transportation, bathrooms, jobs, and doctor offices, just to name a few. Though he'd fought valiantly for America and, we'd much later learn that he'd been awarded many military honors for his military efforts, my father wasn't even allowed to vote. Keep in mind, when he and other black World War II veterans returned home, they were not treated with honor. They came home to the same hurtful discrimination they'd endured before they left. My Mom witnessed the abuse and recognized that the life of a black man was very tough in the 1940's and 50's, especially in the rural South. She also understood and accepted that my father was far from perfect. She attributed it to what he had experienced in World War II and coming home still having to live under Jim Crow laws.

I'm grateful that my mother made the conscious decision not to speak badly about our father. She easily could have made a different decision and tried to turn us against him. Negative statements from her would have had a major impact on how we viewed him. But because she didn't do that and refrained from trying to turn us against our father when we were young, we always loved him. As he got older and needed help, we supported him. We even bought him a car and supported him financially until his death. Most importantly, he knew that we loved him. None of the children ever discussed with him why he left our mother and us.

The Fights Continue

When my father left the family, we were sad but felt that at least the fighting would stop. Unfortunately, the weekend fights continued in subsequent relationships between my mother and the men she dated. My mother, moreover, was no stranger to jail. One weekend, she got into a fight at a local juke joint. The chief of police of our town was called to break up the disturbance. When he attempted to restrain my mother, she hit him knocking him down. This resulted in my mother going to jail, again.

On another occasion, my mother got into a fight with a woman. The woman pulled a gun and shot her. My mother was taken to the hospital but had no insurance. The doctor told her that the bullet lodged in her abdominal area was not life-threatening. He didn't operate to remove the bullet; it remains in her body today. Needless to say, my mother is one tough woman. She fought with my father and won. She fought with other men and women and won. Finally, she fought with a bullet and won that fight as well. But the emotional impact of the fights, tumultuous relationships, and repeated encounters with the law and jail were devastating for us as her children. We were hurt and embarrassed. Our peers would hear about her being put in jail and would make fun of us.

I learned early that the decisions I made personally had a broader impact. My actions not only impacted me; they had a real impact on others as well. If I wanted a positive life, to be perceived with honor, to have self-esteem and a strong self-image, I needed to do my part to make that a reality. I needed to exercise discipline, to be law-abiding, and be my best self to bring pride to myself and family. It all came down to doing unto others as I would have them to do unto me.

Where did these ideas come from? I believe that God's spirit, when the heart is open, can lead us on the good path. We need to listen for *that* spirit and be *that* example for others. I had examples of this "good" in my neighbors, my teachers and my friends. No one was perfect, but many were smart, kind, hardworking and industrious. Despite being born into conditions that are far less than stellar, one can live a life deserving of pride. My message, don't let your status dictate your stature. Be who you want to become; you may just wake up and find yourself in the place you dreamed you could be.

Journey to Success Notes:

CHAPTER THREE

GROWING UP

During the summer months, my brothers and I would get up early and go fishing in a pond that was about four miles from home. First, we'd go out behind our house and dig up earthworms to use as bait. Or sometimes we'd catch crickets to use. We'd put the earthworms and crickets in a can, get our fishing poles made from cane sugar stalks, and walk the four miles down the dirt road until we reached the pond. Normally, other people would already be fishing at the pond because it was closer to their homes. It didn't matter the size or kind of fish that we caught. They all would be cooked and eaten. Sometimes one of the grownups who was fishing at the pond with us would give us a few fish from their catch. Everyone in the small town knew one another so these people knew of our poor situation and were charitable to us.

When we got home, we'd clean the fish and my sister Sender Reatha would cook it, seasoning the fish with cornmeal, salt and black pepper. She'd heat oil in an old iron skillet until it was very hot and fry the fish. That was what we called "good eating." If there was enough, we'd share the fish with our neighbors. To be honest, that was rarely the case.

Skinny Dipping

Another fun memory from my childhood involves skinny dipping. We didn't have swim trunks, so we'd just strip off our clothes and dive in. We swam in the same pond that we used for fishing. This happened in the summer months when we were out of school. My brothers and I would walk to the pond when it got very hot in the middle of the day. Our male friends in the neighborhood usually joined in the fun. The first required task was to throw rocks in the pond to chase the snakes away; or more accurately, to encourage the snakes to dive under the water. You see, we believed that if we couldn't see the snakes, the snakes couldn't see us. And, if the snakes couldn't see us, we couldn't be bitten by them. Go figure! Snakes, even water moccasins, couldn't bite while underwater. Or so we believed. It must have been true because none of us ever got bitten by a snake, and snakes were always in the water when we went swimming. It must also be true that the good Lord takes care of babies and fools.

Blackberry and Muscadine Hunting

Another summer activity was berry hunting. We hunted for blackberries and muscadine berries along the railroad tracks. The tracks ran less than two hundred yards from the front of our house. We'd come home with blue stained teeth because of all the blackberries that we had eaten. If we had a good day finding berries, we would sell them to some of the older people in the neighborhood. But, picking berries was dangerous business: poisonous snakes were often in the bushes with the blackberries. If we saw a snake, we'd just kill it and continue to pick the berries. The muscadine berries grew on vines in the trees. We'd climb the trees to get to them.

We grew up in a time of innocence. I didn't know just how poor we were because the people all around us weren't much, if any, better off than we were. My brothers and I spent a lot of time playing outside because we didn't have televisions, telephones or the electronics of today to help pass the time. When we weren't working, we left the home first thing in the morning and wouldn't return until dusk. We'd just find one another when we got up and commence with planning the day. We'd have foot races, have races pushing old car tires down the dusty road, or just play tag. We played hide and seek a lot. We made our own sling shots; we'd shoot rocks at each other jumping behind a tree or bushes for protection. This game would have a lasting impact on me later in my young life.

Christmas

Christmas wasn't a joyous time. Very early on, my mother told us that there was no such thing as Santa Claus. She did this because she knew she couldn't afford to give us toys or much of anything for Christmas. Yet, we'd wrap up things we already had around the house to give to one another as Christmas gifts. We'd cut pictures of toys and Christmas lights from the Sears and Roebuck's catalog, sticking them on the windows with Vaseline to decorate the windows of our home. On Christmas morning, my mother gave each of us an orange, apple and a stick of peppermint candy. Once we ate our Christmas treats, we'd leave the house to go visit our friends.

There was a ritual at Christmas. If you went to visit someone's home and were the first to say "Christmas gift," they would be obliged to give you a Christmas gift. The gift could be anything, a piece of cake, pie, candy or fruit. We were very good at being the first ones to say "Christmas gift" when we visited a friend or neighbor. We visited our friends so that we could play with their Christmas toys.

We also developed a practice of going to the city dump the day after Christmas to look for toys the white townspeople had thrown away. You see, their kids got new toys and other necessities for Christmas. The city's garbage dump was about four and a half miles from home. My brothers, Ben, Larry and I would get up the morning after Christmas and rush to the city dump trying to get there before the other kids. This allowed us to get some of the good stuff— like old toys, shoes, and clothes. Sometimes we'd even find canned food that had never been opened. Fights at the city dump weren't uncommon. Several kids might simultaneously spy an item, and a race would ensue to get it. That's when the fight would break out. The fights were pretty civilized though; mostly pushing and shoving, no balled fists or weapons were used.

The City Dump ~ A Gold Mine Throughout the Year

We made weekly trips to the city's garbage dump, because there were always treasures to be found. The key was to get there early in the morning before any other kids got there and the contents got picked over. Yes, to us there was *really* good stuff at the city dump like toys, shoes, clothes, etc.

When we reached the dumping grounds, you'd have thought that we'd discovered a gold mine. One year, the athletic department from the white school had bought new shoes for their football team. We didn't have a football team at the black school. Lucky for us, they took the old football shoes, the ones with the cleats, to the city dump. My brothers and I went there, saw those shoes, and thought we'd died and gone to heaven. Once we found our sizes in the pile, we took the shoes, cut off the cleats and wore them as regular shoes. When the soles of our regular shoes would wear out, we would take a piece of linoleum, which is what covered our floors, and put it in the bottom of our shoes to make them last longer. Necessity is the mother of invention.

The city dump was our savior when it came to toys, shoes and used car tires. We used the tires as toys; we'd have tire rolling contests. What fun we'd have! I learned that one man's trash was another man's treasure. I never felt ashamed of visiting the city dump to find what I could use. We considered it surviving. And surviving to live another day was what we did, daily.

Food, What Food?

Food was an elusive luxury in our home. We didn't grow up eating breakfast; there wasn't enough food for that. When I was in elementary school, my mother would give us a nickel a day for lunch. This would pay for a three-ounce carton of milk and four washboard cookies. That was our lunch.

The one big meal that we ate was what we called supper. Supper usually consisted of pinto beans, a little rice, and cornbread. If we were lucky enough to have meat, it consisted of either fish, chicken or pork neck bones. There were many days when one meal was all that we had to eat. We never ate more than two meals on any given day. Many nights, I went to bed hungry. I would dream about food on those nights. As a child, I found that hunger had a taste. It tasted hollow. It tasted bitter. It tasted sour. And, it felt vacant.

We had a neighbor who didn't have children that would give us food to eat. She knew our situation, but my mother still didn't like us going over to our neighbor's house for food. I realized later that my Mom was embarrassed that she couldn't properly provide for us. She told the lady to stop feeding us, saying that she could feed us herself. Our neighbor said okay. But we continued sneaking over to her house and she continued to give us food, admonishing us not to let our mother know. We complied.

Unexpected Food

When I was in the third grade, my teacher asked all of the students to bring in a can of food to give to the poorest family in the neighborhood. I went home and told my mother that I needed a can of food to take to school. She said that we didn't have food to give away, but I pled with her until she allowed me to take a can. I didn't want to be embarrassed by being the only kid that didn't bring a contribution. She finally agreed to allow me to take a can of sardines to school that cost all of ten cents. I was proud that I had something to contribute to the box that was going to be given to help a poor family in our community. My teacher thanked all of the kids for bringing in the cans of food.

Later that day, I got home and pulled off my school clothes. We always changed out of our school clothes before we went outside to play. That evening, there was a knock at our door. It was my teacher with the box. My teacher told my mother, "We know that you are having a hard time trying to feed your family, so here's something to help you." We were so glad to receive that box of food. There was no sense of shame. Being hungry doesn't allow for shame when someone treats you kindly. My teacher never told the other students who received the box of food they'd donated. But, I will never forget it or cease to be thankful for it.

Food Hunting

When I was twelve, I saved enough money to buy a used BB gun. I became a very good shot, and I used the BB gun to hunt. We'd shoot birds of any type for food. My main target was pigeons. There was a church about a block from our house and the pigeons would build nests up in its steeple. There were always plenty of pigeons on top of the church steeple. I would hide, take aim and shoot. I'd manage to get two or three before they'd all fly away. Once home, we'd put them in the pot to remove the feathers. We'd then clean the pigeons, cut them into pieces and place them in the bag seasoned with flour, salt, and pepper. We cooked the meat in a skillet filled with bacon grease. That was good eating for me and my siblings.

I felt bad killing the pigeons because I thought they were beautiful. They were white, blue and some were mixed in color. They shouldn't have had to die like that, but it was a matter of survival for us. We killed birds of any kind, blackbirds, small birds, and larger birds. We would cook them the same way that we cooked the pigeons.

To this day, when I visit parks in the city or on the countryside and see pigeons and ducks, walking about freely, my mind ventures back to my childhood. These pigeons and ducks never would have survived in Gould, Arkansas.

During winter months, my brothers and I hunted rabbits. We used a stick. Again, we made no distinctions on the type of rabbit we would eat. We didn't have real guns. The rabbits were easier to catch when it snowed, because the snow hindered their ability to run fast. Another real delicacy was possum. Men in town would kill them with a gun and sell them in our neighborhood. There was nothing better than a baked possum with sweet potatoes. We liked them because we could eat their bones as well as their meat.

My mother taught all of us how to cook. When we killed a rabbit, we would take it home to clean and cook. Another source of food in the winter was yard chickens. We would grab one, ring its neck letting it flop on the ground until it died. Again, like the pigeons, we would put them into boiling water, pluck the feathers and let them cook. If a neighbor's chicken wandered over in our yard, there was a real possibility that it wouldn't make it back home. Stealing chickens at night was a common occurrence in the neighborhood. It could be a red rooster, black hen or any other color or size, it didn't matter. They all tasted the same when one was hungry.

Overall, I learned from the experience of not having enough food and struggling daily to eat. Growing up there was never enough food for us to eat, but we made do. And somehow we made it through.

This reality inspires me to give to the poor. I practice this by giving to my church and community. Sometimes, when I notice people in line at the grocery store that appear to be less well off, I pay for their groceries. When I see poor children with their parents in a store, I ask their names, what grade they're in, how they're doing in school and, with their parent's permission, give them a twenty-dollar bill. Growing up in an environment of not having enough can either make one bitter or give one a passion for helping the poor. In this way, my life experience has had a positive impact on the lives of others. All things *can* work together for good.

Discipline in the Home

When it came to discipline, my mother had an old school philosophy. She would say, "I brought you into this world, and I will take you out of it if you don't obey me." We believed her. When we were young and did something that got us in trouble, my mother would send us outside to get a "switch" (think of a thin branch) off of a willow tree. She warned that if we brought a switch that was not big enough, she would go outside and get it herself. We never wanted that to happen; she'd bring back what seemed like a limb off the tree to us! The psychological impact of having to get your own means of discipline was worse than the punishment itself.

When we got older, my mother employed another strategy. If we did something worthy of punishment, she would wait until we got in bed. Just as we dozed off to sleep, she would come in with all of the love of a mother, pull back the bedcovers and begin to whip us all with either a switch or a belt. The shock and surprise of the sudden awakening and the accompanying pain to our bodies was unimaginable. We would jump, twist, turn and try to pull the bedcovers back over us. It was even worse if I hadn't done anything to warrant the whipping. However, my mother's thinking was that it didn't really matter who the guilty party was. She would whip us all, rationalizing that we probably had it coming for one thing or another. After a few of these collective whipping sessions, it became clear to my brothers and I that if one of us got into trouble, we were all in trouble and subject to punishment. We decided to monitor each other's behavior working to ensure none of us got into trouble. If one of us witnessed another brother doing something that would get him into trouble, like not taking off his school clothes before going outside to play, we'd make him go back in the house and rectify the situation.

The most difficult part of being disciplined was not the pain of the switch; it was the verbal chastisement we'd receive as our mother was whipping us. I can hear it now: "Didn't. I. Tell. You. Not. To. Disobey. Me," a strike providing the emphasis on each word. I remember it like it was yesterday. Worse than the whipping, she would also talk to us, laying out in clear terms how much we disappointed her by being disobedient. Even today, I hate to disappoint anyone; my boss, wife, family and most of all my Savior, Jesus Christ. I still do my best not to disappoint.

When I made it to the third grade, my mother was still struggling to raise her children without financial help from my father or anyone else. One might say that the Lord works in mysterious ways because by the time I reached the third grade, I was nearly five and a half feet tall and more than capable of going to the cotton fields to pick cotton. We'd stay out of school picking cotton from October through the end of November, sometimes until mid-December. At the end of the third-grade school year, my teacher issued my report card. The word "retained" was written on it. On the way home, I kept looking at that word because I didn't know what it meant. I asked my older brother because he had received his report card, and it had the same notation on it. He explained that I was not going to the fourth grade, that I was being retained in the third grade for another year. Both Ben and I were held back in our respective classes. The emotional impact of knowing that I was not going to be moving on to the fourth grade with my classmates was devastating. I was embarrassed and ashamed that I had failed the third grade. This feeling lingered throughout the summer, especially when someone would ask how I thought I would like the fourth grade. I had to say that I was not going to the fourth grade, that I had been retained.

When school started the next September, many of my classmates who were now registering for the fourth grade kept asking me to come register with them. I had to tell them that I was not going to the fourth grade with them.

I repeated the third grade, and my brother repeated the fourth grade. Though I still missed over two months of school picking cotton in my second time in the third grade, at the end of that school year I was allowed to go to the fourth grade. When I got to the fourth grade, my older brother was still there. He had been retained again because of all the days he missed due to picking cotton.

The same process of my brothers and I missing at least two months of school continued. At the end of my fourth-grade school year, I received my report card. It had a word on it that I now was all too familiar with, "retained." My older brother, who had already been retained twice in third grade and once in the fourth grade, was retained again. Now, I was going to spend my second year in the fourth grade, while my older brother was going to spend his third year there. This put me two years behind my starting classmates, but it put my older brother four years behind his. Again, I was disappointed but not as much as when I'd been retained in the third grade. I think it was because I had experienced this feeling before, so it didn't hurt quite as much. And, the fact that my older brother and I would now be in the same class provided a bit of consolation. My younger brother Larry also suffered the same experiences. He picked cotton, missed school and was retained in the third grade.

The impact of being the oldest and tallest kids in the class was unnerving at first, but we got used to it. The teachers would ask us to help with many chores in the classroom because we were tall and more mature. We weren't the only ones in this predicament, others were retained as well. But because I was so tall, it was pretty obvious that I should be in a higher grade. I learned perseverance from the experience of being held back for two years. It was a hard thing, but I never considered quitting school. I was confident that my mother would've killed me if I did.

Journey to Success Notes:

CHAPTER FOUR

COTTON CHOPPING AND PICKING COTTON

I was eight years old and had grown to be taller than anyone in my class. My older brother, who was ten, was also very tall for his age. This allowed us to work the cotton fields at a younger age than most. We would get up every morning at five o'clock to get ready to catch the truck. The truck would barely stop, merely slowing down enough to allow us to run and jump onto it. The truck would arrive in front of our house at five-thirty, and we'd better be standing outside waiting. If we weren't, the driver would keep going. Missing the truck was a fate worse than death. One morning, I made the mistake of missing the truck. After receiving an emphatic scolding from my mother, she had me working harder around the house for ten hours than I ever would've worked in the cotton field. I never missed that truck again.

My brothers, Ben, Larry, and I picked cotton as I shared previously. We soon became very good at it. We brought the money we made home to our mother to buy food and other necessities for the family. We started to work in the summer, chopping the grass from around the cotton plants. This was called "chopping cotton." This was a ten-hour a day job in temperatures of ninety-five to one hundred five degrees Fahrenheit heat. The pay was three dollars per day. Like on any job, there was a positional hierarchy, and a job that was much sought after. In the cotton fields, that position was that of the "water boy."

The water boy was the worker designated to bring a bucket of cold water to the other workers who were chopping cotton. This bucket had one dipper, and everyone drank from it. Never mind the fact that many of the older people were snuff dippers and tobacco chewers. They'd just move the snuff or chewing tobacco to a different position in their mouths as they drank water from the dipper. Needless to say, some of the remnants made it into the bucket. Once the water boy had served everyone, he went back to the shade tree and relaxed for the next thirty or forty minutes before he had to bring more water to hydrate the workers. This was an essential and highly coveted position. It normally went to the son of the black driver that drove us to the fields. If we rode to the field with a driver who didn't have a son, the job went to the youngest person in the group because it was felt that he/she probably couldn't keep up with the group chopping cotton.

The days were long, but we found ways to entertain ourselves. If someone had a transistor radio, they'd turn it up so we could listen to music as we worked. We listened to Sam Cooke, B.B. King, Aretha Franklin, Ray Charles, the Temptations and the Four Tops. We'd also tell jokes, try to name all the major league baseball players or practice playing the dozens i.e., talking bad about someone's mama. This was a learned skill; you wanted to be known as someone who could really play the dozens. Another skill that one could learn in the cotton field is how to tell time by looking at one's shadow. Many of us got so good at this that we could tell time within minutes of the actual time purely by looking at our shadows.

All of these activities helped to make the day pass more quickly in very hot temperatures. There was another unplanned benefit of chopping cotton in a field. If there was a fruit tree of any kind nearby, we'd avail ourselves of the fruit from the tree during our infrequent breaks. That was always a welcomed and pleasant find.

Hazardous Work

Many days while we were chopping cotton, crop duster planes would fly over us spraying fertilizers or pesticides in the fields next to us. This was such a normal practice that we never paid any attention to it. We inhaled the fertilizer or pesticide that the plane was spreading, but no one ever complained. No one made a report to anyone in authority about the fertilizer being sprayed on us for fear of being fired. There would be no record of any illnesses associated with fertilizer inhalation. We chopped cotton from mid-May to mid-August. It was hard and grueling work, but we were happy to have it as it provided money for food and other necessities for the family.

Cotton Picking ~Winter Work

The cotton was ready to be picked beginning the end of September and this work continued through December. This is also the work that impacted my education the most. We'd start school in September along with everyone else. But once cotton-picking season arrived, we were missing in action; providing income for the family took precedence. We rose early, hopped quickly into our clothes and made our predictable monotonous journey to the fields. In the fall and winter, it often could be cold in the morning sitting on the back of the pick-up truck. Packed with cotton pickers sitting between each other's legs, like sardines in a can, we'd head to the fields. The front cab of the truck was reserved for women and would be so crowded that the driver would steer the truck and one of the women would shift the gears. The trucks didn't have automatic transmissions back then.

On the way to the cotton field, the driver always stopped by a grocery store so we could buy lunch. My brothers and I had an allowance of fifty cents a day. We'd buy a can of pork and beans, a package of crackers, fifteen cents worth of lunch meat (bologna, pressed ham, or Vienna sausages) and a pack of Stage Plank cookies. At lunchtime, we'd buy soda pop for a nickel from the truck driver. He kept them on ice in a tub.

We stored our lunches in the cab of the truck that transported us to the field. Sometimes, however, the unthinkable occurred. Someone would slip back to the truck when we were at the other end of the cotton field and steal some of the lunches. This was devastating to the person who didn't have a lunch to eat. After this occurred a few times, the truck driver would lock the doors to the cab of the truck to keep the lunches from being stolen.

It was important to get to the cotton field early, while morning dew was still on the cotton. This had both a positive and a negative impact. The dew made the cotton heavier and since we were paid by the weight picked, that was a positive thing. However, the dew also caused our clothing to get wet which was cold during fall and winter mornings. This made picking cotton less comfortable. We learned to take the bitter with the sweet.

Picking cotton had another hazard. The sharp edge of the cotton shell pricks the tips of your fingers and those pricks can draw blood. This was normal and expected and it didn't deter anyone from picking cotton. Women would sometimes wear gardener's gloves, but this made it more difficult to get the cotton out of the shell. They'd soon discard the gloves and just endure the pricks. After the first week, calluses would develop on the end of your fingers and the sharp points on the cotton shells would no longer draw blood.

We were paid from a penny and a half to two pennies a pound for the cotton we picked, depending on the farmer. When you filled your sack, you'd throw it on your back and carry it to the scale to be weighed. A number of cotton fields had a man whose sole job was to carry women's sacks to the scale for them. The Whitfield boys were excellent cotton pickers. We could pick over two hundred pounds per day. We sometimes made over four dollars per day, a twenty-five to thirty percent increase over the pay that we received for chopping cotton.

There were ways that the farmer could manipulate the scale to make the cotton weigh less than it actually weighed. And once we became aware of this trick, we'd call him out and he would make some excuse for his behavior and move on. We dared not to challenge him too much lest we be fired on the spot.

But, there were a number of tricks we'd use to add weight to the cotton. For example, at times we would pour water into our cotton sacks or put dirt into them; anything to add weight to the cotton. Once weighed, we were responsible for emptying our own sacks of cotton into a trailer that would later be taken to the cotton gin. When we climbed up into the trailer, if the farmer wasn't looking, we might empty half of the cotton out of our sacks and throw the sacks with the rest of the cotton back to the ground. This meant that we had a good start on filling our sacks up again. All of these tricks caused us to be paid for cotton that we didn't pick. We would be re-weighing the same cotton and getting paid as if it was newly picked. We could have been fired if the farmer ever caught us, but we figured there were always plenty of farmers who needed cotton pickers. Therefore, finding another cotton field to pick in was not a high concern.

One thing experienced cotton pickers knew that those new to the profession didn't, was that one should *never* pick up a pile of cotton found discarded on the ground in the field.

Beneath that nice fluffy pile of white cotton was likely another pile of human waste. There weren't many places to relieve oneself while working in the fields.   There were other activities that took place in a cotton field that had nothing to do with picking cotton. On occasion, one would be walking in the cotton field and come upon two fellow workers using their half-filled cotton sacks as a bed for intimacy. Sometimes they were married and sometimes they weren't. No one was shocked when this occurred in the cotton field. There were plenty of opportunities to trade cotton for sex.   But, what happened in the cotton fields stayed in the cotton fields.

An Unplanned Benefit of Chopping or Picking Cotton

When chopping or picking cotton, if there was a peach, plum or apple tree or a watermelon patch close to us, we would help ourselves to all that we could eat. This was done without the permission of the owner. Our daily allowance for food was fifty cents. We never had breakfast to eat. Therefore, it was a blessing to work in a field equipped with nearby fruit trees. This provided us with unexpected but much needed food to eat. We would occasionally work in a field next to a watermelon patch. Without permission from the owner, we'd eat as many melons as we could.

No Toilets in the Cotton Fields

Perhaps it's obvious, but there were no toilets in the cotton fields. When nature called, you looked for a big tree or a thatch of bushes and that was where you went. If you were picking cotton, you'd take a hand full of cotton and go into the woods to take care of business. If no woods were close by, fellow workers would just turn their backs to allow a bit of privacy within the planted rows a few yards away from them. It was hard and grueling work. Yet, the work provided a certain structure, a rhythm, a feeling of continuity. It was an antidote to boredom and provided a sense of community, social connectedness and purpose.   Most importantly, working in the fields gave us the chance and means to survive. On reflection, I know my life was greatly enriched in those days; and my confidence and self-esteem were forged. I learned one needed to work hard to be successful. If I didn't pick much cotton, I wouldn't be paid much money. But if I worked harder, I would be paid more money. I also learned that nothing in life comes easily; that in making a living, one had to overcome adversity, bloodied fingers, lunches being stolen and no facilities in the fields. But instead of giving up or complaining, I adjusted and made the best if it. The biggest lesson I learned during those sweltering summers, wet autumns, and cold winters was that I had to study hard and complete my education, no matter what or how long it took. Otherwise, I would be doomed to the meager future cotton picking and cotton chopping could provide.   To me, that wasn't a very appealing career choice.

Working Evenings After School

In addition to picking cotton, I had other jobs that I did after school. I worked for a white family in town doing miscellaneous home maintenance. I mopped floors, raked leaves, swept off porches or burned trash in the big barrels out in their back yard. I'd do just about anything they wanted to delegate to someone not afraid of hard labor. For instance, I might notice a few dirt dauber nests up under the eaves of the roof and ask if they wanted them knocked down. I also planted flower beds and vegetable gardens; this was one of my favorite things to do. I learned a lot about planting flowers and vegetables. I used a shovel to dig up and till the soil. And it was a joy to see the benefits of my labor as my flowers and plants grew. It's a pastime that I still enjoy today.

When I worked this job, I was instructed to come to the back door of the white couple's home to get my marching orders. I was not ever to go to the front door. One day, I went to the front door just to see what would happen. I was scolded severely by the man of the house. He reiterated his instruction that I use the back door. This was standard behavior where I grew up in Arkansas. Black people simply were not allowed to go to the front doors of white peoples homes. I was admonished that if I ever went to the front door again, I would lose my job and others would be told of my refusal to follow instructions. I never did it again.

This practice of subjugation and separation extended to many aspects of our society. Water fountains, restrooms, lunch counters and other public facilities provided venues to reinforce the misguided and erroneous belief in blacks that they were inferior and to reassure whites that they were privileged. Our schools, and even where our homes were situated, were impacted by segregation. The railroad track in our city separated the blacks from the whites. And the facilities provided on one side of the tracks verses the other were far from equal. We knew we were expected to take the subordinate position in all things. For example, when riding a bus, one was expected to give up one's seat for a white passenger. When driving long distances, you packed your own food because you were not welcome to eat in restaurants along the highway. You simply stopped along the side of the road when nature called, because though you paid the lawful currency for gas at stations you were not allowed to use the restroom unless the station had a colored toilet as well. As difficult to fathom as this may be today, this was the reality not very long ago in the Jim Crow South. That was just the way it was. To not accept that truth could mean physical and emotional harm, even death, to men, women and children alike. So, for the sake of life, one simply endured and chose to delay temporarily the pursuit of liberty and equality. Change came; it is still coming. God willing.

Thank God For Welfare

My mother tried for years to get on welfare. The government always denied her claim because she was married. My mother and father had been separated for years, and my Dad was not providing financial support. When I was thirteen and in the fifth grade, things finally changed. At last, my mother was able to sign up to receive benefits through programs that provided state and federal financial and nutritional assistance for poor families with children. These programs are better known as "welfare." Once she accepted the fact that my father wasn't returning home, my Mother endeavored to qualify for benefits. She received eighty dollars a month to cover expenses for one adult and six children. It amounted to about two dollars and eighty cents per day for food, clothes, utilities, healthcare, and any other expenses.

The welfare office also provided monthly government food assistance. A person who owned a pick-up truck would travel to the County Welfare Office and pick up the food for the many families that didn't have transportation to drive the eighteen miles to pick it up. If a family didn't have money to pay the driver for the delivery, he would accept a portion of the food as payment. The Government provided cheese, butter, powdered eggs and milk, canned pork and gravy, flour and yellow cornmeal. We were never sure, however, of the precise allotment we would receive each month. If the welfare office ran out of certain foods, we wouldn't get those items. It became very important that the driver arrived early at the welfare office to claim the scheduled delivery.

We'd take the powdered eggs, add a little water and stir them together until it became a batter. We'd pour the batter into a greased cast-iron skillet to cook. The water would separate from the egg batter, and we'd pour it off before we would eat the eggs. The powered milk was also a challenge. We'd mix it with water and stir it with a spoon as vigorously as we could, but it always ended up lumpy. One wasn't pleased when you bit into a lump, there was dry powdered milk inside.

Yellow cornmeal also had its unpleasantries. Within days of opening a fresh bag the bugs had found it. We tried to get rid of the bugs but soon realized the futility of our efforts. So, we'd pick out as many of the bugs as we could and make the cornbread; eating it we knew full well that it contained "added protein." We'd joke that we were having meat and cornbread. On occasions when food supplies were running low, we'd bake cornbread and mix the powdered milk with water making a meal of cornbread and milk. This would fill our stomach and get rid of the hunger pains.

Years later, I visited China and realized that people in many Asian countries ate dogs and cats. Lucky for the dogs in our neighborhood we didn't know that was an acceptable practice; they would have had shortened lives.

Though the money my mother received from the government was minimal, it seemed like a windfall to us. Before we got that, we basically had nothing. Other than the funds we earned chopping and picking cotton, we had no guaranteed money coming into the home. This meant we had no assurance that the bare necessities of life like food, clothing and shelter would be there for us.

One of the requirements for staying on welfare was that the children regularly attend school. That had a tremendously positive impact on my life and on the lives of our entire family. Starting the year I reached fifth grade, my siblings and I did not miss a day of school to pick cotton. Consequently, I was never retained again. My brothers and I still would go after school to pick cotton. We also continued to chop cotton during the summer months.

Welfare helped my family to survive in a time of severe hardship. But we weren't satisfied to remain dependent on the help provided. My mother instilled in us the ethic of being self-reliant, to never depend on a handout to make it in life. We followed her teaching. My experience solidified my belief that while a social safety net is needed to prevent starvation and a life of untold poverty, just as important is the provision of effective education and employment. These are the gateways to hope. One without the other can be an unsavory recipe for failure.

Journey to Success Notes:

CHAPTER FIVE

LESSONS I'VE LEARNED ALONG THE WAY

Helping Others

A couple that was severely visually impaired lived next door to us. Their names were Mr. and Mrs. Gooseberry. Mr. Gooseberry was sixty years old and totally blind. He hadn't always been that way. He lost his sight in an accident around the age of forty. He never provided us with details of the accident. Mr. Gooseberry was a tall and slim man. What little hair he had left was graying. He dressed neatly and always wore cache-colored slacks held up with suspenders with a solid colored shirt of the same color. Mrs. Gooseberry, also visually impaired, was in her sixties, of medium build with salt and pepper hair that she wore pulled to the back with a colored hair tie or ribbon. We didn't know the origins of Mrs. Gooseberry's blindness either. She'd had a daughter before she met Mr. Gooseberry. Her daughter was being raised by her mother. Mr. and Mrs. Gooseberry did not have children of their union.

When I was eight years old, the couple moved into the house next door to ours. I became eyes for Mr. Gooseberry and would take him by the hand and guide him everywhere he wanted to go. We'd go to the post office to get his social security check, to the store to buy food, to church on Sundays and to prayer meetings on Wednesday nights. He was a proud old gentleman. He shared stories with me of his life, his trials and some of the struggles he experienced as a black man growing up in abject segregation and discrimination. He also explained that each day he knew he had a choice to make; to be thankful for his blessings or to grumble and spread discontent about what he didn't have or couldn't do. He chose not to complain and to do what he could to live a positive life.

He told me of how he spent several of his working years loading cargo onto the steamboats in Louisiana and performing maintenance tasks on the docks there. The longshoremen boss would fire bullets at his feet encouraging him to pick up his pace and to work faster. Proud and stubborn to a fault, he reminisced that he'd never work any faster no matter what the boss did to him. When I walked him to the grocery to shop or to other places to handle his business, I'd hold his hand to protect him from oncoming traffic. I'd provide assistance to him in paying the grocer or other bills he needed to take care of. But, Mr. Gooseberry had devised a system of his own to keep track of his money. Each denomination of currency was kept in a separate section of his wallet. He did all of the cooking for he and his wife. This was something that he'd learned to do when he had his eyesight. He would make a fire on his kitchen stove and cook whatever he and his wife wanted to eat.

He had a system of keeping everything in a certain place in his kitchen, flour, meal, salt, pepper, lard etc. He instructed me on how to help him arrange everything in his kitchen. Once arranged the way he wanted it, he never changed it. You almost couldn't tell that he was blind if you watched how easily he traversed in his kitchen. He moved around like he could see. The same system he used to organize the dollar bills in his wallet, he used to organize his food. He'd sometimes bake cookies for us; we loved that.

Mr. Gooseberry also sold soft drinks for a nickel. He kept them in a cardboard box under his bed. Again, he had a system of placing them into a box by flavor, so he knew where to get them when someone wanted to purchase a bottle of what he called "soda water." He was good to me. He bought food for me whenever I took him to the store. Sometimes, he would even buy shirts and cache pants for me to wear matching his clothes. He never had any children, but people often thought that I was his grandson. From Mr. Gooseberry, I learned that life brings about many challenges and that only strong-willed individuals survive. He taught me to never give up but to keep pushing forward. I haven't forgotten the many valuable lessons I was blessed to learn from a blind man with immense foresight and a positive perspective.

Stealing from the Blind

One of the saddest recollections of my young life was taking wood from Mr. Gooseberry to burn as fuel to heat our home. As mentioned, he was a good man who helped me from when I was a boy of eight until I reached the age of twelve when he died. He, like all of the people in the community, cooked and heated their homes with wood stoves. Mr. Gooseberry's wood was stacked on the outside wall of his house. One winter when we ran out of wood, my brothers and I "re-purposed" some of Mr. Gooseberry's wood. To this day, when I think of stealing from a man who had helped me so much, I can barely hold back tears.

I learned a lot from Mr. Gooseberry. We didn't have the benefit of a father in our home, and he taught me many things about life, especially about pride and never giving up. He, like many others in our community, took it upon himself to teach the youth about life and how we should behave. We weren't taught to hate. We were taught to love. To love

Freedom, Identity, Possibility, and America. While Mr. Gooseberry wasn't perfect in all things, he was a good man to me. I thank God that he was a part of my life and of my living memory. I work today, in some measure, to atone for the wrong young Sherman did to him and Mrs. Gooseberry and pray that he looks down upon me in forgiveness.

Approached by a Child Molester

When I was twelve years old, I became the target of a child molester. He was a man that everyone knew was inappropriately attracted to children. There were boys in town that would go willingly to his house to be molested; he bribed them with money. He often approached me, offering me money to pay him a visit. Being poor made me a natural target for him. The money was very tempting. He would take my hand, look at my fingers and say how much he wanted me to come visit him. A few of my friends took him up on his offer; they'd brag about how much money he'd paid them.

The main reason I didn't go was, in my head, I could hear my mother's voice saying, "You know I've taught you right from wrong." Also, I knew that if she ever found out that I visited his place, she would punish me severely. My mother had this saying: "I brought you into this world, and I will take you out!" My siblings and I believed her.

There were so many things that went on in the South when I was growing up that people just didn't talk about, even though they knew what was going on was wrong. Secrets in a small town are not uncommon. But looking back, many adults in town knew about this man. He lived two miles outside the town center on a country road in a one-room clapboard shack. He mowed white people's lawns for a living and had several respected relatives that lived in town. He'd never been married and didn't have any women friends. What he did with young boys was the best-known secret in town. Teaching children to speak up when things are not right is of paramount importance. One thing is certain though, in a small town, a man's failings don't just disappear. People talk. And secrets don't stay secrets.

There were other occasions when it would have been easy for me to do the wrong thing, and I would have done it if not for the teachings of my mother. My fear and respect for her kept me from many a hazard. Mother Dear implored us to never make her ashamed. She said being poor did not make us stupid and certainly didn't have to make us criminals. She'd constantly remind us that if we got into trouble, she didn't have the money to get us out of jail.

Blinded In The Right Eye

During the summer, once the cotton chopping season was over, my brothers and I would play basketball. The basketball goal was a bicycle rim nailed to a post. When I was twelve, we engineered our own homemade slingshots. One unfortunate day, a rock hurled from my older brother's slingshot accidentally hit me in the eye. I fell down in pain but recovered quickly to continue the game of play. Later, I looked at my eye and noticed it was extremely bloodshot. I showed it to my mother. She looked and said, "You'll be alright. Go on back outside and play." So, I did.
My eye continued to swell; so much so that it was nearly swollen shut. My mother put ice on it to help the swelling to go down. After a few days, the swelling decreased but the redness remained. I knew my vision wasn't clearing but not understanding the physiological mechanics of vision, I assumed it was due to the redness of my eye. After about a week, the discoloration cleared, but I still couldn't see. I told my mother. She closed my left eye and asked how many fingers she had up in front of me. I told her that I couldn't see *any* fingers. She said, "Okay, I'd better take you to the doctor."

She borrowed a car and took me to the doctor; not an eye doctor, but a regular family practitioner. After spending hours in the colored waiting room, we finally were called into the doctor's office. My mother explained to him what had happened. He examined my eye but said that there was nothing he could do. The eyesight was lost. He told my mother that she should take me to the hospital in Little Rock, Arkansas' capital city. This was about seventy-five miles from our home in Gould.

Mother Dear had no money or health insurance. But, she called Reatha, one of her younger sisters who lived in Little Rock, to ask if I could stay there until I could get an appointment to see the ophthalmologist at the hospital. My aunt agreed. Again, my mother borrowed a friend's car and took me to Little Rock. A few weeks later, I was examined and, within minutes, was told that there was nothing that could be done. All sight had been lost in my right eye. Amazingly, this news didn't upset me too much. I already knew my sight was gone. What troubled me more was anticipating the ridicule I thought I'd endure when friends found out I was blind in one of my eyes.

I have no doubt that my vision is impaired because we were both poor and without the financial resources to provide for my healthcare. We didn't have the money for health insurance, which is why my Mom didn't take me to the doctor sooner. Immediate access to healthcare could have saved the sight in my right eye. But, again, this wasn't something that was going to stop me from being successful. I decided, thanks in part, to the lessons learned from Mr. Gooseberry, that I would not use physical disability as an excuse to receive pity or special treatment from people.

When I returned home from Little Rock, I vowed to never tell anyone that I was blind in my right eye. In addition to not wanting special treatment, I feared humiliation and being called "one-eyed." I convinced my brothers and sisters not to tell either. Losing sight in my eye taught me more about myself than any other experience that I'd had at that point in life. Sad as it was, it had a positive impact on me becoming who I am today. It encouraged me to never give up and never to seek *or* accept an excuse for not being successful.

Playing Basketball

When basketball season started, I went out for the team and made it as a first-string starter. Back then, no physical fitness exams were required. Therefore, the coach didn't know I was visually impaired. The only problem that I had as a basketball player was with depth perception. Sometimes, this caused me not to be able to catch the basketball. But, through commitment and practice, I made the adjustment. I was a starter on both the junior and senior basketball teams for my school. I made all-district and was named "Most Valuable Player" in a number of games.

When I reached my senior year, I was twenty years old. My age disqualified me from being able to play basketball that year. The coach, therefore, was forced to cut me from the team. I wasn't very good at playing softball or baseball, again due to impaired depth perception and the size of the ball.

I went through my school years without my teachers, coaches or any of my classmates realizing I had the disability. As a matter of fact, when they read this book, many will be shocked by the revelation. This experience taught me how to be diligent in tough situations. More importantly, it taught me not to make excuses for anything that I had no control over in my life. Make the best of it and make lemonade out of lemons.

Segregation/Discrimination

During my childhood, Gould, Arkansas was a small town in the segregated South with railroad tracks in the middle of the town that for generations had separated the whites from the blacks. A U.S. Supreme Court decision in 1954 declared segregated schools unconstitutional, but the educational system in Gould, Arkansas remained largely unchanged for over a decade. In 1964, the Student Nonviolent Coordinating Committee (SNCC) established a regional field office in Gould and supported several African American candidates for the Gould School Board. Black candidates lost the election that year despite the fact that Gould's population was eighty-two percent black. With assistance from the SNCC, a complaint was filed in the U.S. District Court for the Eastern District of Arkansas addressing school facilities, freedom of choice in attending schools, instructional materials, teacher staffing and the money spent per pupil at each school. As a result of the lawsuit, the Gould Special School District was integrated in September 1967. Some of the white parents formed a private academy to keep their children out of the integrated schools. SNCC members also worked in Gould to integrate restaurants and public facilities, and to challenge discriminatory enforcement of local laws.

In my time, Gould had a population approximating thirteen hundred people with a racial makeup of eighty-two percent black and eighteen percent white people. Agricultural jobs predominated, providing employment opportunities for virtually everyone in the area. The majority of black men picked cotton, chopped cotton, chopped beans or shucked corn. Others worked at the only cotton gin in town. The majority of women worked as well. Some were beauticians. If not, they either worked in the fields alongside the men or were employed as maids cleaning the homes or as cooks preparing food for the wealthier white families in the community. The added advantage of being a domestic worker was that their white employers would give old household items and other amenities to them; they'd also frequently donated the clothing their children had outgrown for reuse.

When I was in the first grade, my mother worked as a maid for a wealthy family cleaning their home. Understanding my mother's situation of being financially strapped trying to raise six children, the woman of the house offered my mother some of her children's gently used clothes. Mother Dear brought the clothes home and called all of us together to distribute them. A pair of girl's blue jeans that didn't fit either of my sisters were left over in the pile. My sisters were small, so the jeans were too large for them; my mother told me to try them on. I was devastated, praying that they wouldn't fit.

Back in the 1950's, girl's jeans were different from those worn by boys. Girl's jeans had a zipper on the side, those worn by boys zipped in the front, as they do today. This made it easy to tell the difference between the two. I tried them on, trying to make them *not* fit, I tugged and struggled pretending that I just could not get them on. But my mother wasn't fooled, she said: "Sherman, you'd better put them jeans on and stop pretending they won't fit!"

Unfortunately for me, they did fit. Of course, I would have been taking my life into my own hands had I dared tell my mother that I wasn't going to wear them. The next day, I wore them to school and suffered the catcalls and vocal humiliation. All the kids made fun of me. The boys even followed me to the restroom wanting to see how I'd maneuver and laughed at me more. I'd never felt more shame.

I had another clothing situation when I was in the third grade. We were having a class Play in the afternoon. At lunchtime the teacher told us to go home and change into our nicer clothes for the performance. The Principal and other teachers would be in attendance.

I went home to put on a different colored shirt, but I didn't have anything better than what I was already wearing. When I got back to school, my girlfriend said: "That looks like what you already had on." Wow, that hurt! These two incidents, having to wear girl's jeans and having no clothes to dress up in, had a lasting impact on my life. Once I was able to buy my own clothes, I often "over-dressed" for the occasion. I made sure I looked good, probably to the extreme. But, it helped me feel comfortable, in charge, and in control.

There were three stores in town. The proprietors sold everything from food, clothing and shoes, to small farming tools. The stores would be comparable to a Walmart today, but on a much smaller scale. The majority of the families in the town had credit accounts at the establishments. But, because many blacks couldn't read or write well, they never knew whether they had paid off their accounts or not. The store owners always told them they owed money. When lunch meat was purchased, it had to be sliced and weighed. People knew that a pound of meat looked differently depending on who weighed it.

One of the store owners employed both a black and a white man to work behind the meat counter. When we bought a pound of bologna, pressed ham, or salami there was a clear difference in the pound of meat when the black man weighed it versus when the white man did. We would try to buy meat only on the days when the black man worked, because we knew that he would be fair. Many times, the meats were not properly refrigerated and would have insects flying around them.

There was no such thing as bread being too old to sell, and never was it sold at a discount. Every Tuesday, the store received its shipment of fresh fruit, apples, oranges, bananas, etc. They would put the old fruit outside at the back of the store. We knew that, so we'd venture to the store every Tuesday and go around back to see what we could find to eat. The store owners occasionally saw us, but they never said anything. It also was known that a number of the women that didn't have enough money to pay for food provided "favors" to the store owners as remuneration.

When we purchased clothes, we had to put them in the layaway. We paid weekly on the account until the clothes were paid for. All schools, doctor's offices, restaurants, buses, water fountains and even toilets were segregated. A railroad track separated the white community from the black community. All of the services, stores and banks, etc., were on the "white" side of the tracks. Because most blacks didn't have cars, they walked at least a mile to go grocery shopping. Even doctor's offices were segregated which meant that all of the black patients entered the office by a back or side door into segregated waiting rooms. Blacks were seen by the doctor when there were no more white patients waiting to be seen. This was the norm in those days, and we didn't spend our time complaining or worrying about the situation. We spent the time in the waiting room talking, sharing news, local gossip and exchanging recipes with each other. Mind you, we only visited the doctor when it was an absolute emergency, meaning when one of the home remedies used didn't cure the ailment. We didn't go to the doctor for mumps, fevers, measles, colds or pneumonia. These illnesses, and many more, were treated by homemade cures, or what today would be called holistic herbal medicine. Most home remedies involved liquor mixed with dried corn shucks.

Even the delivery of a baby was performed by a community-based midwife without formal training. The midwife in our community was Mama Ada. She was a medium build light-skinned old woman. She delivered just about every child in the area. All six of the Whitfield children were delivered by Mama Ada.

Routine preventative dental care was non-existent. If a tooth got an especially big cavity or was unbearably painful, my mother would show us how to pull it for ourselves. Alternatively, we went to the regular doctor, not a dentist, to get it pulled. Our cavities were never filled. When we were very young and our baby teeth had to be pulled, we were taught to take a piece of thread, make a circle, tie it over the tooth and snatch it out. This process worked every time.

I didn't understand the problems of endemic segregation or the resulting wrong that was done to black people by its continued enforcement. I thought it was just the way things were. As I got older, I learned that segregation was wrong and emblematic of a system designed to deny basic civil and human rights to a whole group of people based on their race. The discriminatory practices served as a means to subordinate and deny rights to minorities; institutions were built around enforcement of disparities that served to keep us in poverty, less educated and in menial jobs. While I now can understand these things, when living it in my maturing years, I had more important concerns to worry about. You know, concerns like: Food. Clothing. Shelter.

The Ku Klux Klan in Gould

In Gould, Arkansas, the Ku Klux Klan was a well-known organization. This was true for most southern towns in the United States. My mother had a credit account with one of the grocers in town. She'd go to the store, buy food on credit and pay the bill when she received money at the end of each month. One day she went to the store and saw, prominently displayed, a notice announcing the time and location of the next KKK meeting.

Mother Dear was offended and raised her concerns with the store's owner. Predictably, he waived her off and ignored her. She told him she was going to pay off her bill and wouldn't shop at his store anymore. She worked to convince other blacks to do the same, and they followed her lead. The "boycott" was effective. It wasn't long before the store's owner had no one to buy the stale bread, spoiled meat and other expired food items that he had been selling to customers at regular prices.

Everyone knew the KKK was a prominent force in our town, but now they had demonstrated a total lack of respect by so blatantly publicizing their meetings. This event launched my mother's activism and support of civil rights actions in our community. She stood up against injustice regardless of the consequence. Little did we know the severe percussions my mother's willingness to fight for civil rights in our community would cost her and our family down the road.

Desegregation of Schools

In 1967, the desegregation of schools reached Gould. I was in the ninth grade. Some students were given the "freedom" to choose which school they wanted to attend. Our choice was between attending the all-black school or the newly integrated white school in town. Three percent of the best students were chosen to attend the white school. Because I was now an honor student, I was one of the students chosen to move. Like everyone else I was afraid on the first day we integrated. None of us had much experience living or associating with white students. Our social interactions with whites were minimal, and the limited interactions we had were not usually positive. Many white parents took their children out of the public school transferring them to a new private "academy" that had been quickly constructed to avoid their children having to attend school with black students.

Upon enrollment in the integrated school, we were met with discrimination. We received little encouragement, indeed many of the teachers showed us clear disdain. It would be an absolute understatement to say that the learning environment was difficult. I went from being an A and B student to failing, making D's, F's with an occasional C. This was the experience of the majority of the transferring students.

To be sure, our failure could be attributed partially to the new environment in which we were placed and to the fact that our previous schooling hadn't been up to the same standard we were currently experiencing. In truth, our academic training was behind that of the white students. They had been studying from more advanced books than those provided to us. The prevailing practice in the Arkansas school system had been to provide minority schools with the older obsolete books when new books were purchased for the white schools. This gave the whites in the majority populated schools a clear advantage. While this might explain some of the gap, the gap shouldn't have been so vast that I would go from making A's and B's to D's and F's. Some of the failures were a reflection of the harshness of the teachers and their preconceptions of the inferiority of their new students.

By the middle of the first semester, my mother met with the school Principal in an effort to understand how an honor student's performance could drop so suddenly. Rather than deal with the issue, the Principal told my mother that she and other parents could choose to return their children to the all-black school. It was crystal clear to my mother what was happening. She understood the diversionary tactic for what it was, and she was not confused about what was taking place. But, concerned with the disquieted and down-cast spirit I was exhibiting mid-semester, she had me transferred back to the black school.

While this was, in many ways, a backward step, the experience provided us with the first-hand knowledge and experience of just how far behind we were in comparison to white students. I committed to study harder than I ever studied before. I started making straight A's. Two years later, many of the white students had either been transferred to another all-white school in a different city or enrolled in the private academy. The two Gould schools, therefore, were merged into one integrated system.

Now, I was back with the white teachers and the few white students that remained. Most black teachers in our school had been relegated to being assistants to the white teachers; one of the negative impacts of school integration. My quandary, could I still make straight A's with these new teachers? I did. At the end of my senior year when it was time to select the valedictorian of the class, I had the highest grade-point average of anyone in the combined school. However, there was another student attending the integrated school that was a close second. The teacher that organized the senior class graduation ceremony decided we should be co-valedictorians. I was, however, given the honor of giving the valedictorian speech.

My experience attending the white school awakened my scholastic aptitude and focus. I was driven to study harder. Previously, I'd been a student that, without much effort, could get A's and B's. Confronted with stiffened competition and higher standards, I didn't measure up. But, the experience helped me to understand that to be truly competitive, I needed to be able to compete with *anyone*. My competition wasn't only with those with whom I was comfortable and knew well. I needed to be able to excel in a much broader context. I needed to be able to swim and compete with different fish in the bigger pond. That required I work harder and truly apply myself to doing the very best I possibly could do. I began applying this learning in all areas of my life. I pushed myself harder. It started with setting goals for myself; putting plans in place to achieve my goals and then taking actions that would make my goals a reality. I wanted to be the very best that I could be, so I set my standards high. Excellence was my goal. My advice to you, dream you can touch the sky; then start working on a plan to make it happen.

81

Journey to Success Notes:

CHAPTER SIX

MY MOTHER THE CIVIL RIGHTS ACTIVIST

In 1965, my mother was elected president of the Gould civil rights organization. The name of the organization was Gould Citizens for Progress. Its membership was made up of the women, men and children of our town. The goal of the organization was to fight against discrimination in the local area with a main emphasis on fighting for voting rights. On one occasion, my mother and others held a March to protest for the right to register to vote in Gould as opposed to having to travel eighteen miles to Star City to exercise that right.

A newspaper reporter from Pine Bluff, Arkansas, came to Gould, took pictures of the marchers and wrote an article about the protest. My mother's picture was on the front page of the newspaper and the following article was written:

Courthouse at Star City is Picketed

Pine Bluff Commercial Southeast Arkansas Bureau, 701 N. Main Street, Monticello
Star City: Nine Negroes picket...all members of Gould Citizens for Progress, an organization formed especially to protest voter registration policies of R.A. Goyen, Lincoln County clerk- demonstrated for about two hours at the courthouse here yesterday.

Goyen opened a temporary voter registration office Monday at the Lions Club Community Center in Gould and announced that the office would be open five days. Registration in Gould came to an abrupt halt Tuesday night when the Gould Lions Club voted to deny the clerk further use of the building.

A spokesman for the Lions Club said no reason for the action was discussed before the Tuesday vote. The Negroes alleged that voter registration was shut down in Gould because, on the first two days, more than 300 Negroes and only 16 whites were registered.

Goyen said that his office registered 225 voters in Gould on Monday and Tuesday, but he had no record of the race of the registrants. The Lions Club, he said, "had a perfect right to want their building," and added that, when the use of the community center was denied him, "I didn't have time to find another place."

All further registration, Goyen said, will be in his office at the Lincoln County Courthouse. The clerk had planned to open two other field registration offices but he said, "I am not through with it after this."

The demonstrators came to the courthouse at 1:30 p.m. yesterday. For about two hours they stood on the sidewalk near the north end of the building and held signs. The signs said:

--"Promised 5 Days and Got Only 2 Days."

--"Bring Voter Registration Back to Gould"

--"Can the Lions Club Push Our County Officials Around?"

--"Let Us Register in Gould"

--"We Want a County Government That Keeps Promises"

A spokesman for the demonstrators, Ola Bynum, 28, of Gould, said Gould Citizens for Progress is not a civil rights group. She said that the organization was formed "day before yesterday (Tuesday)" and, she added, the purpose of the group is "to get registration back in Gould."

Miss Bynum said Gould Citizens for Progress has "30-40 members—I don't know exactly."

While my mother and the protesters were unsuccessful in getting voter registration moved back to Gould that year, they took a bold and courageous stand for voter's rights. Clearly, this is a fight that continues today.

Paying the Cost for Taking a Stand

My mother gained a reputation as a troublemaker based on the courageous positions she took against the store owner that posted the KKK notice in his window and her stand for voter registration. We believe it was because of these brave stands that she was removed from the welfare roll that same year. Being a lawful recipient of the aid, the government provided meant our family could eat, keep a roof over our heads and pay our utilities. We had limited resources and what we had was insufficient to maintain the necessary dietary requirements for our family. Simply put, we often went hungry. A civil rights lawyer in Little Rock, Arkansas, took the case to get my mother's benefits reinstated. The case went on for nearly a year. When the hearing was set, the government claimed my mother was removed based on rumors that she had a man living with her in violation of the welfare rules. There was no man living with us. But, the old saying of: "white makes right" was at play; meaning, if a white person said something, that made it true, no questions asked, no other proof necessary.

In the year my mother was ineligible for aid to provide for her dependent children, we found ourselves back in a familiar situation. We didn't have the necessities needed for daily living. During that time, my mother periodically received money in the mail from unidentified sources to help her as she fought her case. This blessing allowed us to eat. Sometimes an offering would be taken up by the Gould for Citizen Progress Committee. My mother also worked at a local restaurant and, with the permission of the proprietor, would have one of us come to the back door of the restaurant where she'd give us a pot of food to take home to eat. We'd walk two miles carrying the hot pot to our home. It was obvious to the friends and neighbors we passed on our way just how poor and desperate we were. Through the eyes of a child, it was hurtful for others to see our struggles. Finally, the civil rights lawyer won the case. He was successful in convincing the welfare board that my mother did not have a man living with her. Her benefits were restored. Everyone believed the government's actions were taken in retaliation against my mother for standing up for her rights against the store owner and for fighting for voter rights.

I find it ironic, even today, that the government will help women with children *only* as long as no man lives in the home. As soon as the father or other male shows up, the mother's eligibility is rescinded. If she removes him, the government reinstates the benefit increasing her income for each child that she has, as long as the father's not there. It doesn't take a genius to figure out what's going on. Seemingly, it's a system set up to perpetuate itself; keeping women and their children in a generational cycle of dependency and poverty. The system makes it profitable for mothers to keep having children as long as the father maintains his absence. And as a result, children grow up without a father and, of course, the process repeats itself over and over again.

Please understand, the welfare system was not put in place to provide benefits for minorities. To say this would perpetuate the myth that blacks are its sole or predominate beneficiaries. This is not the case. The system providing aid to dependent children is active in every State of the Union, and the majority of those on the welfare rolls are white. The statistics and demographics reflected in them are clear and widely available. But, many are surprised to learn this fact. One need only look at the traditional depiction of the "Welfare Mom" to understand why. The singular portrayal of a sad, typically over-weight, black woman poorly dressed and surrounded by many black children standing in line comes to mind. The truth is, the majority of welfare recipients are white. One only need check the welfare rolls for a State where very few minorities live, like in Vermont, Idaho, Colorado, Oregon, Maine, Utah, Indiana, Minnesota, or North or South Dakota. Or, in States where minorities may live in the larger cities, just take a look in their suburban or rural counties to see that Welfare Offices are present and serving predominantly white citizens in said counties.

There are racial disparities that reflect and provide clear indicators of the systemic problems present in our society. We need to work to address them. But poverty, wherever it is found, is a problem as well. To address any problem, we must first acknowledge that it exists. If we fail to do so, we have little hope of finding a solution. Racism and poverty are two problems that are related but not identical. I believe that if we work together to address them both, we can make tremendous progress as a nation. The old saying that "the rising tide raises all boats" makes sense here. Yes, tidal change is required to erase the neglectful scourge of poverty and racism many have endured.

I thank God that my mother worked to instill in us the understanding that poverty and racism are problems we need not accept as life sentences. Don't misunderstand me, there is nothing wrong with the *person* that happens to be poor or in need of help.   But, they needn't be satisfied with the conditions in which they find themselves. Just like cancer is a disease that needs eradication, both racism and poverty are the enemies we need to address with fervor. There is nothing wrong with the person that has cancer; it is the disease that requires treatment. People may live in poor conditions and need help. A multi-level cure is needed. We should dismantle policies that have supported racism and done little to reduce poverty. And, simultaneously, on the individual level, we must remember that we needn't be *satisfied* living that way with racism or poverty. Each day make the personal decision to better your own circumstances and that of your family. Don't just wait for society to change; you live the change that you want for your life. That is how true change is born, nurtured and thrives.

Courthouse At Star City Is Picketed

Pine Bluff Commercial
Southeast Arkansas Bureau
281 N. Main St., Monticello

STAR CITY — Nine Negro pickets—all members of Gould Citizens for Progress, an organization formed especially to protest voter registration policies of R. A. Goyen, the Lincoln County Clerk—demonstrated for about two hours at the courthouse here yesterday.

Goyen opened a temporary voter registration office Monday at the Lions Club Community Center in Gould and announced that the office would be open five days. Registration in Gould came to an abrupt halt Tuesday night when the Gould Lions Club voted to deny the clerk further use of the building.

A spokesman for the Lions Club said no reason for the action was discussed before the Tuesday vote. The Negroes alleged that voter registration was shut down in Gould because, on the first two days, more than 300 Negroes and only 16 whites were registered.

Goyen said that his office registered 255 voters in Gould on Monday and Tuesday, but that he had no record of the race of the registrants. The Lions Club, he said, "had a perfect right to want their building," and added that, when the use of the community center was denied him, "I didn't have time to find another place."

All further registration, Goyen said, will be in his office at the Lincoln County Courthouse. The clerk had planned to open two other field registration offices but, he said, "I'm not going through with it after this."

The demonstrators came to the courthouse at 1:30 p.m. yesterday. For about two hours they stood on the sidewalk near the north end of the building and held signs. The signs said:

—"Promised 5 days and got only 2 days."
—"Bring voter registration back to Gould."
—"Can the Lions Club push around our county officials?"
—"Let us register in Gould."
—"We want a county government that keeps promises."

A spokesman for the demonstrators, Olab Bynun, 28, of Gould, said Gould Citizens for Progress is not a civil rights group. The organization, she said, was founded "day before yesterday (Tuesday)", and, she added, the purpose of the group is "to get registration back to Gould."

Miss Bynun said Gould Citizens for Progress has "30 to 40 members — I don't know exactly."

She said the group intends to picket "until they come back to Gould." She said she did not consider yesterday's protest a civil rights action.

Another demonstrator, Gloria Jean Foote, disagreed. She said she thought the registration office was closed because more Negroes than whites registered.

Picket Protests Clerk's Policy

It was a long hot summer in 1965 when Lucy Dale Whitfield, President of the Gould Citizens for Progress, took a stand. She fought for the rights of the local citizens to register to vote in their local community of Gould, rather than in Star City, Arkansas. The 18 mile trek from Gould to Star City was a barrier to local citizen voter registration; the requirement was born out of efforts to suppress the African-American vote

Lucy's letter to her brother Richard Dale, aka Red, telling him about her fight to protect Arkansas Voter Rights. Lucy said she fought for the hopes and future of her five children: Benjamin, Sherman, Larry, Sender-Retha and Naomi.

Gould Ark.,
July 22, 1965
Dear Richard & Dale
Not much to say but
to let you all hear from
me we all are doing ok
and hope that you all
likewise. Red will you
please write me I want
to hear from you all.
Red I am sending you all
a paper, to let you no
what we are trying to do
here in Gould. This is
my picture down the
... where we
Picket in Star City
... in front of ...
from your Sis
Lucy Whitfield
P.S. over
I am the President of
our organization

Journey to Success Notes:

CHAPTER SEVEN

ONE STEP AT A TIME

When I was eleven, we lived next to the "colored" high school. One Saturday afternoon, some boys from the "other" side of town came by our school with BB guns and shot out many of the school's windows. The following Monday, the principal called the police to report the vandalism. The police came and picked me up, along with my brothers and several of our friends. We all were placed in the police car. As he drove us around town, the officer said: "I know you boys shot those windows out in the school. Just tell me how many windows each of you shot out, and I'll take you back home. But if you don't, I'll have to take you to jail. You'll all be sent to reform school." We were scared to death just being in a police car. When he said that we would be put in jail and sent to the reform school, we were petrified. One of my friends said he'd broken three windows, another said that he'd broken two. Finally, my brothers, Ben, Larry and I said we'd also broken some of the windows.

The policeman took each of us home. Our mothers were told that they would have to stand trial for their boys breaking out the windows at the school. When the policemen left, my mother asked what had happened. We related the sequence of events to her; that the policeman had come to school, made us get into his police car and said that he already knew that we were the ones who'd broken the windows. When we denied it, he threatened to take us to jail. So, Joe said that he'd broken three windows, Calvin said he'd broken two and Freddie said he'd only broken one. Then, the officer told my brothers and I that we had better confess too or he was going to drop Joe, Calvin and Freddie back at their houses and take us to jail. We'd gotten scared and told him that we'd broken out two windows each.

Our mother admonished us that we should never lie, even if the truth gets us into trouble. We hung our heads in shame. The hearing was to be held in two weeks. My mother and the three other mothers went to the hearing together. None of them could afford a lawyer. Judge Butcher came in and took his seat on the bench. He asked my mother and the other women whether they had anything to say before he issued his ruling.

My mother spoke up. She said: "Judge Butcher, our boys did not shoot out those windows. We are all on welfare and can't afford to buy our boys the BB guns that were used to shoot them out." She went on to say: "the white boys in town shot out those windows." The judge, at this point, told my mother to watch her mouth. He asked my mother, "Who were the white boys that you say shot out the windows?" My mother said, "I don't know, they all look the same to me." The judge said, "Lucy, I told you to watch your mouth."

It was a bold thing in those days for a black person to accuse a white person of doing anything wrong. Yet, my mother continued her defense saying: "Judge Butcher, I'd rather pay fifty dollars in the right rather than ten cents in the wrong. None of us has a husband, and we don't have any money to pay a fine." Judge Butcher thought for a while and said: "Alright, you all can go home, but I don't want to see you back here again." As the women walked home, they all thanked my mother for speaking up for them. My mother told them: "Any of you could have done the same thing." But, in truth, it takes a lot of courage to speak up, even when you know you're right.

This is another example of my mother standing against the odds and winning. She had a reputation for speaking her mind and not backing down from any situation. The judge could have put her in jail, merely for speaking up to defend herself. She was willing to go to jail if necessary. I was and am proud of my mother for standing up for us. She is my hero. The lessons I learned from my mother are clear: Tell the truth, even if it causes you to get in trouble. And stand up for what is right.

Gold Teeth ~ A Family Tradition

My mother has had a bridge of gold teeth in the front of her mouth for as long as I can remember. Her top four front teeth are gold; initially, she had it done as a fashion statement. Later, when she lost her teeth and had to get dentures, she had the gold plating included. My father, several aunts, uncles and many neighbors wore the fashion of the day as well. In the summer before I reached the ninth grade, I saved enough money to have a gold crown placed over one of my front eye teeth in a half-moon design. My brothers, Ben and Larry, and the eldest of my sisters, Sender Reatha, soon followed suit. It may seem strange, but it was the "in" thing to do; kind of like the tattoo craze of today. All of my classmates complimented me on how good I looked, especially the girls.

Gold crowns were an emblem of prosperity for many people during that time. For the Whitfields, it was a matter of family tradition. Seeing black people in the south with gold teeth was as common as white on rice. Though people might struggle to eat and pay their light bills, having gold in their mouths was a priority. I kept the gold through high school, college and even the beginning of my working career. Indeed, I had gold until I was thirty-seven years old. Interestingly, no one ever suggested that it might be time for the gold tooth to go.

That is, not until I began dating my current wife, Paula, over thirty-eight years ago. She sensitively asked why I had it. To be honest, I didn't receive her query too well. No one had ever asked me about it, not even my first wife. And besides, my mother had four gold teeth, my dad two and my two brothers and eldest sister had one each. I interpreted her question not only as an interrogation of me, but of my entire family and its values.

But Paula's a very smart lady. She saw how strongly I'd reacted, so she let it go for a while. Later she said, "You know when people see your gold, they attribute a lot of things to you that you aren't aware of. Things that are not true." I asked for clarification. She explained that stereotyping was at play, and that while it might be unfair, its negative impact was there nonetheless. The initial impression one gives is a lasting one. Gold in Gould, Arkansas might project success, but in other regions in our country, inaccurate as it may be, having gold teeth signaled a lower-class mentality, lesser intelligence and was not seen as professional. Simply put, she told me that with one look, indeed, as soon as I smiled, decisions were made about me, wrong decisions that left lasting impressions. Impressions I might not like. It struck me that she was being kind when she said I didn't look intelligent; it was a nicer way of saying I looked dumb. That's how I took it at the time anyway.

But on reflection, my eyes were beginning to open. I slowly began to understand the difficult truth. Six months later, I visited the dentist and had the half-moon replaced with an open-faced gold crown. This meant that I only had gold around the edges of my front tooth. When I next visited my girlfriend, I was expecting a big reaction like, "Wow, you did it; you got rid of the gold!" That's *not* what she said. She acknowledged that while removing the half-moon improved my appearance, she didn't understand why I hadn't taken the opportunity to rid myself of the gold entirely. Though I knew she was right, it was complicated. Honestly, I was afraid. I didn't know how I would explain the change to my family.

For nearly a year, I kept the gold crown. But once enlightened, one cannot ignore new knowledge and understanding. I was bombarded with images on television, print media and on the big screen of people sporting gold crowns. The impression and stereotypes they sought to evoke were now clear to me. I was a smart, educated, professional and ambitious young black man. I decided that I wanted to present myself to the world as such. I got rid of the gold crown.

To my surprise, I received a multitude of compliments from everyone I saw. Many now freely relayed their thoughts on the negative images and stereotypes that having gold portrayed and evoked, particularly in the business world. When I got back to Arkansas for a visit, the family's reaction was varied; some approved, others didn't, and most said nothing. But on the next trip home, my older brother had gotten rid of his gold crown. Others soon followed suit. But, many family members still sported gold, after all, it was the family's tradition.

What's In A Name

In the ninth grade, my mother's youngest brother, Hules Dale, or Uncle Buck, as we referred to him, invited my brother and I to come to Chicago to stay with his family for the summer. My brother was nineteen, and our uncle was able to get him on at the Coca-Cola Bottling Company. I was only seventeen and, thus, not yet eligible for a job in the factory. The law required individuals to be at least eighteen years of age. But, I needed money for school clothes and to provide for the family at home. I looked for a company that would hire me and found one. The only identification required was a social security card; I used my brother's card as identification. On the job that summer, my name was Ben Whitfield. The job was at the cookie company where my father had been employed when he'd first moved to Chicago. He had long since left the company, but the proprietors remembered him and hired me. He'd left a positive and lasting impression at the company.

That summer, I heard many amusing stories about my father from the people he'd worked with and for at the factory. The women seem to have the most stories, but they all loved him. Everyone was very helpful to me, based mostly on the respect they had for my father. The only issue was getting used to answering to my new name. People would be yelling "Ben" repeatedly and I wouldn't respond; I think they thought I was hard of hearing. After a bit, I got used to it. I worked all of the overtime that I could get. And, employees could eat all of the cookies they wanted. I ate a lot of them the first month but soon got my fill of them.

As I look back, I reflect on my desire to work so badly that I was willing to become someone else. At the age of seventeen, I was willing to do whatever it took to pull myself out of poverty. The next summer, my older brother and I went back to Chicago. Because I was now eighteen, my uncle was able to get both my brother and I on at Coca-Cola. Once my younger brother Larry got a bit older, he came as well. We all continued to work summers at Coke through high school and college.

Later on, as an adult, I considered my actions. How far was I willing to go to get ahead? How much of myself was I willing to compromise for money or success? While I'm not proud of what I did that summer, I understand it. It's what drives immigrants to cross borders for work; it's what encourages athletes to blur lines and rules of play to win. The experience gave me perspective and helps keep me grounded today. I can't cast dispersions on others when I know I'm far from perfect.

If honest, I don't think many need look too deeply within themselves or their own life experiences to acknowledge that "but for the grace of God, there go I." Living in poverty shouldn't be looked upon as a badge of courage; however, it needn't be considered a scarlet letter either. But, ignoring poverty or allowing it to persist can serve as a mirror on one's soul and the soul of our society.

First Suit of Clothes

When it came time for high school graduation, neither my brother, who was graduating with me, or I owned a suit. My mother couldn't afford to buy them for us, so we wrote our Uncle Buck. He had a wife and three children of his own and tirelessly struggled to keep his head above water; but he bought us suits for graduation. These were the very first suits my brother and I owned, and man did we look sharp. We felt even better. Sometimes just looking good provides the spark needed to light the fire within. We wore those suits proudly, and they spurred in us a confidence and resolve that we *could* make it. We could succeed against all odds.

It might seem odd that we could be seniors in high school never having owned a suit. But, we didn't often go to church or attend social events requiring such attire. We'd had sports coats, but never a suit. I do recall that we once rented tuxedos for senior prom. But, wearing that first suit was the most memorable event in my young life. Like the Temptations said, I was on "Cloud Nine."

College Years

I'd graduated valedictorian of my high school class and was determined to enroll in and graduate from college. My brother Ben and I enrolled at the University of Arkansas at Pine Bluff, formally known as AM&N College, in 1969. No one in our family had before gone to college. But, we were driven to get a college education and suffered no illusions that it would be easy. Our mother didn't have the means to offer financial support; our father was still missing in action. But again, our Uncle Buck and Aunt Ola saved the day. They made us welcome in Chicago during the summers. Uncle Buck lined up jobs for us at Coca Cola. Without that, we'd never have had enough money to matriculate. During the school year, I worked to pay my college tuition, housing and other expenses. We couldn't afford to live in the dormitory, so we rented an off-campus room from an elderly lady. She was a soft-spoken but tough spinster whose house and fortunes had seen their better days. The home was in need of repair, but she kept it clean. The front yard was full of the poor man's paraphernalia, pink plastic flamingoes, multicolored ducks, gnomes, birdbaths and flowers.

Our room had one bed. My brother and I slept there, just like at home. We had trouble making enough money for our meals. We went home most weekends where our mother fed us and sent us back with whatever food she could spare; it was seldom enough. Four more young students lived in the house. When our food ran out, we helped ourselves to theirs. Once one of the guys realized someone was stealing from him, he removed the labels from his can goods surmising that no one would take his food if they didn't know what was in the can. That didn't stop us. We'd eat whatever was found in the can we opened. Sometimes, we'd avail ourselves of the campus meals served at the cafeteria without showing a pass. We weren't proud of ourselves for what we did, but even the Bible says that a man will steal if he is hungry. *Proverbs 6:30*

We got jobs at a place that provided storage for the cottonseed used in the region. There we shoveled seeds away from the area where the grain elevator dumped them, moving them into the containers used for storage. The work was hard but provided the cumulative benefit of building both muscle and money; a powerful combination. The work conditions were dusty and hot. The seeds, dust and the sweat generated from our labors combined to make a muddy broth that rolled down our bodies. Later, I got a job working at a soda bottling company where I washed bottles "returned for deposit" to the grocery stores. We seldom had enough money to pay rent, so we did chores for our landlady. We'd paint walls, mow the grass, clear the brush and basically do any jobs she needed doing to cover for our rent.

At the end of our second year, my brother left college to get married and find a job to support his family. He later returned and got his college degree. I resumed the established summer trek to Chicago where I'd live with my Uncle and Aunt and work at Coca Cola. I took all of the overtime I could get. In my second year of college, I learned that the State would pay my tuition; a benefit that resulted from me being visually impaired in one eye. This was a huge help. This cycle of working and struggling and struggling and working continued through graduation. But, the benefits I gained aren't lost on me. Indeed, I wouldn't change a thing, for to change one thing might cause me to miss out on the many blessings I now enjoy.

I majored in Business Administration and minored in Accounting. My fiscal situation provided ample incentive for me to study hard and not fail a course. I couldn't waste the time or money failing would engender. The school's library was my home away from home. While many of my friends partied and had a good time, I hit the books. I kept my head down and finished college on time with honors. I graduated and was debt-free when I did; that was another great accomplishment.

Journey to Success Notes:

CHAPTER EIGHT

CAREER BEGINNINGS~GENERAL MOTORS

In 1973, General Motors was one of the companies that recruited me at the University of Arkansas. I interviewed with a number of impressive companies, e.g., State Farm Insurance Company, Ford Motor Company, Sears & Roebuck and a few others. But, General Motors was offering the most money and, thus, most captured my interest. After successful completion of the first round of interviews, the company flew me to Danville, Illinois. This was the first time I had ever flown on a plane. The interviews went well, and I got the job. To be honest, I understood little about what my job actually was going to entail. My sole concern was what my salary was going to be. I accepted their offer and returned to the University to complete my senior year.

I was hired to work at the Central Foundry Division of General Motors Corporation in Danville, Illinois. My job title was Supervisor, and I was the third black ever hired to work as supervisor in the plant. My first challenge was finding a place to live and getting proper clothing to wear in a work environment. I didn't have money saved to help with the move. But thankfully, I learned that a guy named Frank Aldridge that I had seen a few times around campus also had been hired by General Motors. I contacted him and told him my situation. Through some connections, Frank arranged for me to stay with an hourly employee that worked at the plant. The hourly employee offered to let me move in with him and to delay my payment of rent until after I'd received my first paycheck. I accepted his generous offer. When I moved in, he also loaned me a few hundred dollars to buy proper clothing to wear to work. At the time, I didn't know it wasn't considered proper for a member of management to live with an hourly employee. It's a good thing that I didn't; I had no money and was short on other options.

My first day was one of introductions and filling out the usual paperwork. I was given a full tour of the plant. To be honest, the best way to describe it was that it was like walking through the gates of hell. The sheer intensity of the operation is difficult to describe. The heat generated in a foundry strikes you full force when you enter, like a wide hand pressing and clutching the center of your chest.

The Danville Plant was a gray iron foundry. Here the work environment was dark, smoky, dirty and dangerous. The plant was vast; you couldn't see the end of it, only blackness relieved by showers of sparks and bubbling vats of liquid fire. Molten metal glowed white hot in giant ladles as they rocked along the overhead monorails. Metal clanged against metal, conveyor belts rolled, machinery clanked, clattered and churned. I asked myself what I had gotten myself into. Most of those working in this area were men, but there were a few exceptions. All of the employees wore safety glasses, steel-toed shoes, earplugs, reinforced safety gloves and long-sleeved shirts even in the summer due to the molten iron constantly being poured to fuel production. There was little sitting down on this job. One always had to be watchful for a spark, a spill, a fall or a slip, because life and limb depended on it.

Central Foundry used scrap iron, purchased mostly from a local source that was brought in by rail to the plant. The scrap iron was melted in furnaces called cupolas. The molten metal was poured into sand-casting molds. Once the metal solidified in the sand-casting mold, it went through what is called shake out. A vibrating conveyor shakes some of the sand away. The remainder was removed in the Finishing Department. We made brake rotors, intake manifolds, water pumps, master cylinders and many other iron parts used in manufacturing cars.

In the summer, the temperatures in the plant could reach one hundred thirty degrees Fahrenheit. It wasn't as bad during winter months. Safety was a constant concern and point of focus. One misstep could have tragic implications. For example, if an employee slipped and fell into the cupola, there would be nothing left of them to see or bury. Yes, I wondered if I had stepped from the frying pan into the fire; but I was mindful of the fact that in comparison to working the cotton fields, at least I was being paid well.

After the first day of cursory introductions, I was assigned to shadow a supervisor for a week to learn his job. The job involved supervising thirty-two hourly employees in the Finishing Department of the plant. The work in Finishing was much better than in the melting area. The hourly employees, fully cognizant of my being a neophyte supervisor, took advantage of the situation. They didn't perform their assigned tasks, took extra breaks and called the union steward on me for imagined violations of the union contract. By the end of the week, I'd learned more than I ever thought I could have in a week. This was true trial by fire. I learned more by experience on the job than in any other way. After three months on the job, I went to Saginaw, Michigan for a week of new supervisor training. I felt it was three months too late.

I was delighted when I received my first paycheck; you couldn't tell me anything! I felt I'd achieved a portion of the success I'd been working toward. My first paycheck reflected more money than I'd ever had in my possession at one time. Once deposited into my checking account, the first thing I mailed was a check to my mother to help her and my younger siblings. This is a practice that I continue to this day.

Little time was wasted in my quest to collect items that I believed reflected my newfound success. Within six months, I'd purchased a new car, a Buick Electra 225, neither an inexpensive nor fuel efficient choice. I also purchased more than my fair share of fine clothes. One could say I was living "high on the hog." And they would have been right. I wasn't saving much money, but I did join the company's stock and profit savings program. This was a program through which the company would match, dollar for dollar, contributions made into a 401K Savings Account, up to six percent of one's salary. If needed, employees could borrow from this account at a very low-interest rate, and the interest paid actually was credited to your own account. So, there was no real penalty from taking money out of the account. I found myself doing this a bit too often though, a clear sign that I wasn't managing my money well.

To say that the relationship between GM management and the United Auto Workers Union (the "Union") was confrontational would be a significant understatement. Neither party trusted the other. Though Union and management used the same cafeteria, they never ate or sat together at the same table. Management and Union personnel used separate restrooms, showers and even had separate parking lots. This separation reminded me of the divisions and segregated conditions I'd grown up within the South. Profanity was the language of choice on the shop floor. Remember, I'd earned my stripes playing the dozens in the cotton fields of Arkansas. Indeed, one was considered a good supervisor if you honed the art of using disrespectful expletives when addressing the hourly workers. I was considered a superb supervisor.

The Power Of Unions

I supervised approximately thirty employees, give or take a few, in the Finishing Department. The daily schedule laid out the number of iron casting pieces my employees were to grind. Employees used a grinding wheel driven by an electric motor to remove excess metal from the castings, so the end product was of the required dimensions. The castings were made from gray iron and were used to form water pumps, power steering pumps, exhaust manifolds, intake manifolds, rotors and many other parts that went on the engines of GM cars and trucks. Some of the parts weighed as much as forty pounds. Employees needed to be physically fit and to have sufficient manual dexterity to pick up, maneuver and grind the excess metal off a given component.

Employees, based on their seniority on the job, could choose the casting that they wanted to grind. I had several women assigned to my department and most of them had less time on the job than their male counterparts. This meant that they were left with the toughest castings to grind. The Union's contract prohibited me from making lighter-duty assignments to employees based on gender. There was much resistance from the men when women first started working in the plant. All grinding jobs in my department were piece rated, which meant that the employees were expected to grind a certain number of castings per hour. The Union's contract provided that once an employee completed the required number of pieces designated for the shift, they could stop performing that activity and be entitled to receive pay for eight hours of work. In Union terminology, they had "made rate." Once an employee "made rate," the remainder of their time could be spent doing clean-up work in the area. They didn't need to perform any more work for the entire shift.

Especially adept employees could complete eight hours of grinding work in between four to six hours. This meant that they were done for the day, and I couldn't ask them to do any more work for that day. This created problems. Once a worker completed their eight-hour rate and cleaned up their area, they were free to go to the locker room until the end of the day. Some would arrange to have one of their buddies punch them out. They'd leave the plant, go home, to a bar or wherever. Of course this was illegal, but some would get away with it. And, because most female foundry workers were on the harder jobs due to seniority, very few of them could grind the required number of pieces for the shift. They'd end up working for the full eight-hour shifts.

Absentee Workers

One of the most prevalent problems faced by supervisors was employees either showing up late or not showing up at all. It was hard to meet the production schedule if you didn't have all hands on-deck. And, to make matters worse, the absenteeism increased the stress on those that did show up. It created big problems for the Union as well, because they were tasked with defending the employees disciplined for failing to show up for work. The problem was systemic.

My standard practice was to issue a written warning to those that missed or showed up late to work on a regular basis. The warning was placed in their personnel files. If the warning didn't do the trick, I'd give them a day off without pay. If that didn't modify their behavior, I issued an order of two days off without pay and so on. Our hope was that hitting them in their pocketbooks would engender improved compliance. This method of discipline could continue until thirty days off without pay was reached. The next disciplinary order would be discharge. But due to the strength of the Union, a discharge rarely ever happened.

Negotiations, Church And Three Little Pigs (not centered like others)

I had an employee that was poised for a two-day suspension without pay. The employee was distraught; he didn't want to lose the money. His Union representative pled his case emphasizing his dire financial circumstance outlining every sob story you could imagine. I made an offer that if the employee would attend church the following Sunday and bring me the church bulletin evidencing his attendance, I would rescind the discipline. He agreed. The following Monday, he provided the church bulletin. To be honest, I knew people who attended the church and verified that he'd actually attended and stayed for the whole church service. His work attendance improved.

Another one of my employees owned a small farm. One day his neighbors called the plant and left a message indicating that the employee's pregnant sow had gotten out of the fence and he was needed to help retrieve her. It wasn't uncommon for calls, claiming so-called "emergencies" to come in on a Friday afternoon requiring employees to leave early.

When I received the message, I conveniently neglected to give it to the employee. The following Monday, the employee called his Union representative to report that I had failed to relay the message and that the sow had died. He claimed the company should pay for the sow and its three unborn piglets. I asked for proof of his claim, but none was provided. I denied the claim. The Union appealed the grievance to the next step which was my boss. He asked me to resolve the claim indicating that he was inclined to compromise because I hadn't given the employee the message. We settled the grievance. I paid for the cost of the allegedly dead sow and two of the supposed three piglets that she was carrying.

Frequent Layoffs ~ No Big Deal

We often had to layoff of hourly employees. A layoff occurred when the company shutdown a part of the production. The layoffs typically were temporary and could be for a week, two or even several months. The reduction in work force orders were issued based on car and truck sales and the resulting reduced demand for the parts we manufactured. Interestingly, an announced layoff was not a particularly worrisome event; indeed, many employees were happy to get the reprieve. The reason, employees received up to ninety percent of their pay while laid off. This was not a good business decision, or in the long-term best interest for General Motors or the employees. But, the Union had immense power and because of that power, they were successful in getting such terms negotiated into the contract. Such terms led to many of the competitiveness issues General Motors and other U.S. based automobile manufacturers faced in the coming years. But, at the time, employees "benefited" from the leverage the UAW had in negotiating terms that protected Union members.

After five years, I was promoted to Assistant Superintendent. I managed a shift and led a team of between six and eight supervisors. The number on my shift could range from one hundred fifty to two hundred fifty employees. It was a big responsibility. For the next fifteen years, I was an Assistant Superintendent working on a variety of shifts in virtually every department in the plant.

The relationship between blacks and whites in management could be described best as lukewarm. While at work, we conversed, got along and got the job done. Outside the formal workplace, there was very limited social interaction. We just didn't run in the same social circles. Few attended the same places of worship. People knew little of their colleagues' families or the lives they led outside the plant. And, there were few *real* friendships. Again, this circumstance was reminiscent of relationships that I had experienced in the South. I had always been told that the racial relations were different between blacks and whites in the North; but to my surprise, in my early experience, there was really little difference. The racial divide was not as obvious as it was in the South. We worked together and got paid well. And, there was diversity in management. But, the seismic divide was still there.

Just A Few Trials

When my first wife and I met, I was a senior and she was a junior in college. She was a tall, shapely, attractive and poised young woman. She'd grown up in Rosston, a small town in the southwestern part of Arkansas with a population of about two hundred and sixty-five people. Like me, she'd come to Pine Bluff to pursue her education at the University of Arkansas. She majored in education and was preparing to become a high school teacher. Culturally speaking, her family was definitely a few steps up the societal ladder from mine. Her mother was a teacher and had quite a bit of status in their small community. She was career-focused and had a good head on her shoulders.

After dating for six months, we decided we wanted to spend the rest of our lives together. We got "unofficially" engaged which meant that we'd committed to be married but that I hadn't put a ring on her finger yet, so it wasn't considered to be official. Of course, I didn't have the money to buy a ring so we agreed that *that* formality would have to wait until I could afford it.

Upon reflection, it is clear that neither of us really knew what we were getting into. We didn't know one another well at all. As typical college students we knew what we both liked; you know, things like fried fish, smothered chicken, collard greens and dancing. We both enjoyed looking good and being surrounded by nice things. But we hadn't really taken the time to understand one another's goals, aspirations and inner-most desires. In the short time that we dated, we had quite a few arguments that, in retrospect, should have given us both pause. But, we moved ahead blindly and unaware of the challenges we soon would face.

I remember one weekend while we were still in college, she went home for the weekend. When she returned, she was wearing her old boyfriend's class ring. And we had a big argument about it but moved on with our relationship without really resolving the reasons behind the conflict. After I graduated college, I moved to Danville, Illinois, to take the job I'd landed with GM. She had a year to go before completing her studies.

I guess absence made the heart grow fonder, because the time apart increased our affections for one another. Right after she graduated the following year, we were married. For a time, albeit a very short time, things were happy; ignorance was bliss.

She moved to Danville, and we set up housekeeping in an apartment. Upon arrival in the city, she got a job at Hyster Corporation as an account representative. The following year, she landed the job she really wanted as a teacher at the Danville High School. Things went well in that first year. She made friends with a group of young teachers and adjusted well to our new, seemingly secure, lives together.

Because of our jobs, we made enough money to qualify for a mortgage and purchased a home in the impressive northern section of town. We were the first African Americans to move into the established upper-middle class neighborhood, which raised a few eyebrows at work and in our social circles. The house was a light-colored brick ranch that sat on a quiet and charming tree-lined street. It had three bedrooms, one and a half baths, a spacious living room with a fireplace, a nice eat-in kitchen, a large backyard complete with an awninged patio and an attached garage. We were excited, and our respective families were proud of us.

Obviously, setting up a new home comes with added expenses. We bought new furniture, hung draperies, acquired the necessary furnishings, painted and papered the rooms. We also had to buy pots, pans, cutlery, a lawn mower, vacuum cleaner and other household equipment for handling the routine maintenance. We both had new cars, and my wife needed to enhance her student wardrobe for her new professional job. Very quickly our monthly outlay began to exceed our income. Before long, our wedded bliss began to unravel.

It wasn't just the financial strain. We had disagreements about my going out with friends too often, about what we'd each spend money on, about my not going to church. Truly, we argued about anything and everything. Looking back, she was right on most accounts. You see, in the year before we'd married, I'd lived footloose and fancy free. I'd established a practice of going out with the boys. It was fun. For the first time in my life, I had the financial means to go out with friends, to pay for drinks and dinner and not have to worry about how I'd eat the next day. I saw no reason to change the pattern. So, when we got married, I continued to go out a lot with my male friends. My money management skills were non-existent; and going to church was not even on my radar.

I hadn't grown up watching a positive or functional marital relationship, putting it mildly. Indeed, because my father wasn't present, I had no true model of what a husband should do or how one should treat his life partner. Loving one's wife unconditionally wasn't something I knew anything about. My wife's background had its issues as well. Her parents divorced early, and her mother had two additional unsuccessful marriages. Neither of us understood what it meant to be in a committed relationship. And I was, by no means, a choir boy.

Back in those days, there was no such thing as a mentor. I learned about being a husband by watching my married friends stumble through their relationships. Some were good, but most not so much. I will be the first to acknowledge that what I learned from them did not serve me well. My wife was a Christian; early in our marriage she attended church services pretty regularly. I was what astute Christians jokingly refer to as a "CME Christian;" my attendance was limited to Christmas, Mother's Day and Easter. After a while, her commitment to regular attendance at church began to wane. The decline in her attendance signaled the sure and steady deterioration of our relationship.

Acrimony

We argued frequently, but we never resolved our issues. We'd just negotiate a cease-fire for long enough to replenish, reload our weapons and the incessant quarreling would begin anew. It was at this juncture that we decided to try to have a child. Not a smart move; a clear absence of wisdom. We wrongly thought adding a baby to the already strained family dynamic would work to solidify our already troubled relationship. We had difficulty conceiving and visited a fertility specialist to help the process along. At our doctor's recommendation, we began making charts on the calendar, taking her temperature to pinpoint ovulation and timing our sexual activities to improve the chances of conception. When her monthly cycle would arrive, the painful emotional impact this was having on the both of us was abundantly clear. The fertility challenges did nothing to improve our relationship. As a matter of fact, things got worse.

One evening, we got into our typical argument about my comings and goings. This time, however, she ventured into the kitchen and pulled a knife from the drawer. I asked, "What are you doing?" She lunged at me with the knife, and I threw up my arms. The knife sliced a deep gash in my arm. I was bleeding badly. This was the first time that one of our conflicts had turned physical. Mind you, I'd grown up with domestic violence. It was a customary occurrence in our home in my early life. I'd witnessed it first-hand between my mother and father and had made a pledge that I would never engage in it. Standing there in my kitchen with blood streaming down my arm, I had to make a split-second decision, was I going to keep my vow? I did.

I rushed from the house and drove myself to the emergency room. On arrival, I was rushed to a trauma room for medical attention. It was first thought that a vein had been severed. Thank God that wasn't the case. Once they got the bleeding under control and multi-stitched my arm, they began questioning me on how the injury happened. I lied and said that I'd accidentally cut myself. Inspecting the positioning of the wound, hospital personnel didn't believe me and said they needed to call the police. I stuck to my story indicating that if the police were called, I would tell them the same thing. They relented and didn't contact law enforcement.

I returned home. She apologized. We theorized that her hormones were elevated and out of wack and moved on. For a time, I straightened up. Occasionally, I even went to church in an effort to keep the peace and please her. But it didn't last long. Soon, I resumed my nights out with my friends.

One day, during a now routine episode of discord, she told me that "a friend" had informed her that I had been seen partying with "the boys" and several single women. The story wasn't true. But, I asked who'd spread the gossip. It took several efforts, but eventually she told me the guy's name. He was a fellow teacher and coach at the high school where my wife worked. He also moonlighted as a local part-time minister. I was livid. The next day, I ventured to the school to confront him. The security present in schools today was not in force. I was directed to his classroom. Once I found him, I asked him if we could find a private place to talk. He was no fool. He correctly suspected why I was there. He attempted small talk in an unsuccessful effort to diffuse the situation. Undeterred, I asked him why he was spreading false rumors about me to my wife. He denied the accusation saying, "Come on brother, I would never do anything like that." I didn't believe him but felt confident that I'd made my point and that he wouldn't do it again.

Six months later, my wife was pregnant. She carried the baby to term, and we had a beautiful and healthy baby boy who we named Sherman Louis. He brought us joy. But, as is often the case, his arrival didn't remedy our marital problems. Indeed, the difficulties we'd had not only continued, they worsened. Our lives were not destined toward the traditionally fabled fairytale ending. There was to be no "happily ever after." Our lives together were instead pre-destined toward a sad end.

Journey to Success Notes:

CHAPTER NINE

DIVORCE

Our marriage continued down its rocky path. One day, I came home unexpectedly. On entering the front door, my wife appeared nervous and was in a state of undress. That wouldn't have been an issue but for the fact that I caught a fleeting peripheral glimpse of someone running out the back door. I ran after him. My wife called the police. When the police arrived, the man came from behind the bush on the side of the house where he'd been hiding. I was shocked to see that it was the same man that I had confronted at the high school.

To put it mildly, I wasn't pleased. I yelled and screamed every profane word I could recollect. Putting it nicely, I called him everything but a child of God. The police instructed him to leave. And he left our property on foot. I was shocked to find an unfamiliar car parked inside the garage. It was his car, and the keys were still in the ignition. This further infuriated me. I surmised that this was their routine plan to prevent detection from neighbors or other passersby. I took his car keys, got in my car and drove to his house. I gave the keys to his wife and told her what I had just found. I invited his wife to come to get their vehicle from my place. By this time, tears were rolling down my face both from hurt and anger.

His wife apologized to me, because she could see my brokenness. Later that day, she came over and got the car. When I got home, I packed some clothes and checked into a local hotel. Before I got settled at the hotel, I stopped at a liquor store and bought a bottle of Crown Royal whiskey. I spent the night crying and drinking. I called some friends telling them what had happened. Few were surprised. Evidently, many in town already knew of the affair.

In truth, I was distraught. While I went through the motions and tried to act like I was moving past it, the pain simply would not go away. This was a hurt more profound than any I had before experienced. I turned inward and lost myself in alcohol. It reached a point where I just didn't care about anything. I even quit my job at General Motors. When this happened, my boss, God bless him, called and left numerous messages for me to come in to talk to him. I didn't answer the calls. I didn't call him back. A week later, I received a personally delivered telegram from the plant manager. His name was Jim Wheeler. He had heard that I was not answering my phone or returning any messages. In the telegram, he indicated that he'd been told that I was having some personal problems. He implored me to come in and talk to him.

After a few days, I called his secretary and scheduled an appointment to meet with him. As we talked, tears started to roll down my face. He gave me his handkerchief. I don't remember much of what we said. But, he did ask if I'd found another job. When I told him "no," he strongly encouraged me to take a few days off and to come back, at least until I found another job. I took his advice. After a few days, I called my boss and told him that I was returning to work. I'm so thankful for the mercy my boss and the plant manager showed me during that dark time. I shudder to think of how much more devastated my life could have been had they not cared and given me that period of grace.

I was in such a sad and desolate state. They knew that I was really struggling in my personal life, and that it was my hurt and confusion that had caused me to quit. It would have been easy for them to take a different tactic, to not help me to see the bigger picture. Instead, they chose to give me time, help me to reflect, regroup and find the mental space to fight another day. For that, I will always be grateful. It wasn't just my marriage that was in trouble, it was my entire life. I was heavily in debt, didn't really like myself, and was on my way to becoming an alcoholic. My marriage was over, but because of them at least I still had a job.

After a time, my life began to change. My wife and I would speak by phone occasionally, but the conversations always ended with me raging about what had happened. It made matters worse when I learned that the affair had been going on for quite some time. That was the last straw. One day while my wife was still at work, I borrowed a friend's truck and moved all of my things out of our residence. I also took a bedroom suit, a lamp, a love seat and recliner chair. She wasn't surprised, because I'd not slept with her since finding her with her friend.

I moved from the hotel and settled into a nice two-bedroom apartment. I bought new living room furniture and set about outfitting my new place in typical bachelor-pad style. I bought an oversized "Pit" styled sofa, and a nice dining room set. My friends provided recommendations on local divorce attorneys, and I enlisted one for help. I advised my wife, in no uncertain terms, that I was filing for divorce and that I wanted to move forward with a legal separation. She tried to reason with me to slow down, asking that we let things cool off for a bit. She professed her love and a willingness to work on things, but my mind was made up. In my mind, there was no going back. I'd made the decision, and it was time to move on with my life.

A year and a half after I'd moved out of the house, our divorce was final. She was given custody of our son Sherman Louis, but I was given liberal visitation rights. My memories of the time spent with Sherman Louis during that time are bittersweet. He was an adorable child; his smile and laugh lit up any room. He brought joy to my heart, and I hated that my time with him was limited because of our separation. I'd pick him up on Fridays and keep him most weekends. My now ex-wife insisted that I call before I came by to pick him up though. I soon figured out why. Her affair and clandestine meetings with her friend continued.

A Changed Life ~ Coming To Christ

After a year or so, though I was back at work, I was not fulfilled. I was unhappy. Dysphoric. Depressed. Put simply, my life just wasn't right. My heart hurt, literally; and I felt an emptiness to my very soul. My new friends Jack Daniels, Crown Royal, Beefeater and Smirnoff provided a fleeting but temporary relief. But when I'd awaken from a night of drinking and partying, the desolate feeling was still there. I'd reached the point where I no longer cared whether I lived or died.

It was then, when I'd arrived at rock bottom, that I remembered conversations I'd had with my grandmother as a child. She'd been dead for over twenty years at this point but still I could recollect how she'd speak of a man from Galilee. This man raised the dead, gave sight to the blind, blessed the lame to walk and enabled the dumb to talk. My grandmother spoke with such conviction about this man from Galilee that I thought Galilee was a city in northern Arkansas. I wondered whether this man, Jesus, could do anything for me. My self-esteem was at an all-time low. But, I wanted my life back and concluded that since I had tried nearly everything else, why not try Jesus?

There was a revival in progress at a local church on a Monday night. I decided to go. Frankly, one part of my mind was telling me to go, but the other was holding me back. After engaging in an internal debate for some time, my better-self won out. I made my way to the church and sat in the very back pew. I listened attentively to the preacher's sermon. When he finished, the choir started singing the hymn "Amazing Grace." When they got to the verse that says, "Amazing grace, how sweet the sound that saved a wretch like me…," this got my attention. I'd heard once that our view of God has everything to do with those who taught us about Him. Our image of Him often reflects images of them or what they'd taught us about Him. Growing up in the South, I'd been taught that for a person to be saved, one needed "to get their life right;" and one needed to "sit on the mourners' bench" until they could "feel the spirit of the Lord." If the spirit "really" hit you, you were supposed to jump up, dance around, turn flips, run up and down the church aisles and generally make a lot of noise and raise a big commotion.

I had a positive view of God. But, it was skewed somewhat by what I'd been told about the actions one needed to take to be accepted by Him. I knew that my life wasn't right, but I wasn't prepared to turn flips or run up and down the church aisles. However, when the choir sang that Jesus was in "the wretch saving business," I got excited. As they finished the hymn, I raised my hand. The minister asked what he could do for me. I told him that if the choir sang one more verse of Amazing Grace, especially the part that said his grace would save a wretch like me, I would come down and accept Christ. He said, "Sing church;" he encouraged the choir to sing the song again and again until I walked down the aisle. I gave my hand to the preacher, and my heart to God.

My life was in shambles when I came to Christ. I was a broken man, I was in debt and, candidly, I didn't like myself. The Holy Spirit drove me to read the Bible daily for hours. A fervent hunger to learn more about Jesus developed in the core of my very being. I went to church every time the doors were opened anywhere in the city. I gave money to the church, but only in cash. I didn't want to write a check for fear it would bounce.

I had a new life; one that could come only from accepting Jesus Christ as my Savior. He accepted me just as I was, worthless, and when I had no love for myself. It was then that the Father called me his beloved. I was on my way to hell, but he pulled me up from the depths of my despair and set me in heavenly places in his Son, Jesus. I knew I couldn't pay God for what he had done in and for me. He'd literally given my life back to me. While I understood nothing could buy his love or pay for my salvation, I wanted to serve him. I joined the choir, the usher's board and, in time, I was asked to be a church trustee and even invited to be a deacon.

I had to keep reminding myself that I was saved by God's grace and not because of my work in the church. But, Jesus didn't just change my life spiritually, he changed my daily walk as well. This transformation even extended to how I began to feel about my former wife. I wasn't angry anymore. No longer was I driven to say hurtful things or to constantly relive the events that had caused the disintegration of our marriage. By grace, I'd been given a second chance. I made up in my mind to not waste it.

I started off by setting new goals for myself. I charted a path to getting out of debt in five years. I enrolled in a Dale Carnegie Course that touted its ability to help build self-esteem and to improve the public speaking skills of its students. And, I decided to go back to school for my Master's Degree. Finally, I'd realized that the only person that could save me from me was me. Going through life blaming others for my own mistakes was just silly and dumb, a non-starter. At this, the lowest point in my life, I decided to take charge of my destiny.

Whenever I share my story, I give my ex-wife and her clandestine friend credit for my becoming a Christian. You see, without the intense pain and hopelessness I'd experienced, I'm not sure I ever would have taken the necessary steps to become a Christian. Because of that realization, I wouldn't change one thing that happened; not my first failed marriage, my poor financial decisions, or my reckless and undisciplined drinking. Nothing. The result of it all was that I became and remain a child of God. That, truly, is the most important thing I've done in my life. So, I thank my former wife and her clandestine friend. They impacted my life in an eternally positive way. For that, I am forever and exceedingly blessed and thankful.

Several years later, I ran into him, the one I'd chased from my home. By now, my marriage was long over. The divorce was final. My former wife and son had moved out of state, and we'd established our separate lives. To my surprise, the hurt and anger that I'd had for him too was gone. I walked up to him, greeted him and shook his hand. My change of mind and heart can be credited solely and totally to the love of Christ.

My ex-wife Sandra moved to Texas after the divorce. She had extended family there and was able to find a job teaching near Dallas. We'd arrange our son's transfer for my holidays with him at her family's home in Arkansas. He spent all of his summers with me. Often, she asked why I couldn't have been the person I'd now become when we were married. She'd changed too. But, my interpretation of what she was trying to communicate was if I had been, she wouldn't have had the affair. I don't know if that is true or not. But, I agree with her assessment of me and the character I displayed during our marriage. I wasn't the husband I should have been.

Nearly seven years after my divorce, I remarried. This time, I was more mature and had a better understanding of what it meant to be a husband. Paula and I dated five years before we married. My first wife and her new husband had one child together, a daughter. Unfortunately, that marriage too ended in divorce. To make matters worse, she developed sarcoidosis. She managed the effects of the disease well for several years, even going into remission for a period. She continued to teach high school developing an excellent reputation in the city where she lived and taught. She eventually married again; this time to a high school coach. But, the symptoms of the sarcoidosis returned. She had several medical procedures performed to alleviate her symptoms but, just a few months after her third marriage, she suffered a brain hemorrhage. She died suddenly sitting at the desk in her office shortly after arrival that morning at school. Her death was a shock to everyone. No one realized her illness was that serious; especially not her children or her new husband.

Upon receiving the tragic news, my wife Paula and I flew immediately to Texas to be with my son. By this time Sherman Louis was twenty-one years old. Sandra, my wife Paula and I had long since developed a positive and comfortable relationship. We understood the freedom of forgiveness. Paula frequently accompanied me when I'd go to pick up my son for our visits. She even developed friendships with my ex-wife's mother and extended family. Being one of the first to arrive after her death, we jumped in to help. Sandra's husband was in shock, as were the two children. Paula stepped up to assist in planning the funeral and even wrote the obituary.

The funeral was well attended. She clearly was a much-loved teacher. Her church, work colleagues and current and former students showed up in large numbers. It was a little strange for me. The three men she'd married were present at the funeral. We were all very polite to one another. Her parents preceded her in death, but several uncles and cousins were there as well. We, meaning Paula and I, knew them all; whereas the other two husbands clearly didn't.

After her death, Paula and I continued to provide the necessary support for my son, both emotionally and financially. Paula is an attorney, so she helped in the handling of the estate and life insurance proceeds. The adjustment went as well as one could expect. The loss of one's mother or father, whenever it happens, is never easy. But, my son continued to grow and mature into a wonderful young man. He learned from the mistakes he saw while growing up in a twice divorced household. He is one of the most solid and committed men I know. He is a committed Christian having accepted Christ at a young age. And, he is focused, above all, on his faith and on being a strong and devoted husband, father and ever-present support for his family. He's married to a lovely woman, Shajohnia, who is also a teacher. They have two beautiful children, Destiny and Louis. And, thanks be to God, we all have a great relationship.

Good Life Changes

The experiences and mistakes in my first marriage taught me a great deal. I knew that most of them resulted from a lack of knowledge of what "being married" really meant. I hadn't had many examples of what a true love entailed or how to work past hard times. That said, my whole world changed when I met Paula.

Our first meeting was fortuitous. Paula's family moved to Danville when her father was transferred there from Jackson, Tennessee by the Quaker Oats Company. She attended Danville High School and was a cheerleader back when the school system enforced racial quotas limiting the number of African American girls that could be on the cheerleading squad. This was a highly coveted position. And, as the only black on the squad, she immediately became a member of a small elite group of young ladies in Danville. Everyone knew her. But, being new and pretty in the close-knit community, making friends wasn't easy. The Collier family, a large family in town, was immediately open and friendly to her. They understood the resentment others in town often projected on newcomers, especially those that attained coveted positions. Several Collier girls had been cheerleaders, pompettes and even Homecoming Queens in Danville. Paula shared much in common with them as she'd been a cheerleader throughout grade school in Chicago and high school in Jackson, Tennessee as well. She'd also made the Homecoming Court in Jackson, Tennessee, the first African American to gain that honor at Northside High School.

I credit the friendship Paula developed with the Colliers for our first meeting. Paula came home for the summer after her first year in law school and called her friends Unita and Lolita Collier to see what they were doing for the weekend. They told her that they were going to a Corvette Club party at the Laura Lee Fellowship House. She wasn't keen on going to the party, but they convinced her to go anyway. The gathering was one sponsored by a group of African American professionals that worked at GM and drove Corvettes. And, yours truly was one of its founding members.

Paula came with Unita Collier, Lolita Collier, Johnnie Young and Deborah Grant, a group of ladies we affectionately referred to as the "wolf pack." They were a beautiful group of professional young women that went out together often, and they looked out for and protected one another. These friends are responsible for bringing Paula into my life.

As she approached the door of Laura Lee Fellowship House, I noticed her immediately. She was just plain beautiful. She was slender, shapely and had bright beautiful hazel eyes, her hair flowed over her shoulders and her skin looked soft and was the color of honey. She wore burgundy slacks with a cream-colored top with an intricately embroidered flowered bodice. Her sleeves were short showing off her tanned and toned arms. But, what I noticed immediately was that she had come uniquely prepared to our "bring your own bottle" affair. Unlike others that came carrying brown paper bags, on her arm she carried a black and red leather case that I soon learned held her fifth of black labeled Johnnie Walker scotch. She was a woman after my own heart.

I saw something else too. A strong family resemblance to a man I knew from General Motors. Her father, Arthur Taylor, Jr., had left Quaker Oats and joined General Motors. She had what I would come to recognize as the Taylor walk. She, her Dad and four brothers all have it. As she approached the entry over which I stood guard, I asked: "Are you Art Taylor's daughter?" She said "yes." And, with that one "yes," my new life was started. Art, her father, had told me about his children. He was a father of five, and he was proud of them all. I knew his daughter was in law school. In my mind, she had the two qualities I loved, physical beauty *and* brains. The ultimate combination. I initiated conversations with her throughout most of that night. Unbeknownst to Paula, a few of the ladies that I simultaneously was dating were present at the party. I'd decided earlier that evening that it would be best if I stayed clear of the party and just manned the door. I didn't want to bring attention to the fact that I had several girlfriends at the party; asking *one* of them to dance would have just caused a scene. But, to be honest, once I saw Paula my thoughts were elsewhere; it was all over.

Paula brought a light, a warmth, a clear direction to my life that I had never before experienced. She was like the sun; and it was as though my heart felt a gravitational pull toward hers. I can't imagine that all men love their wives like I love Paula. If they did, we wouldn't get much work done. Or, maybe we and the world would be at peace. My life's focus changed that night; after our first date it changed irrevocably. I knew the novelty eventually would wear off, but it captured me just the same. I smiled and laughed like never before. It was like we always were meant to be together and always would be. I knew it from the first. To me, it was as if our lives had sprung up from the same place and would return there in the end. I had to convince her of that mind you; she wasn't as smitten immediately. But I worked to do that using what I coined as "the full court press." I took her to lunch every day. When we first started dating, I was working second shift at the plant. That meant I worked from three o'clock in the afternoon until eleven o'clock at night.

Paula worked as a law intern at the Vermilion County Prosecutor's Office for the summer. I would pick her up each day for lunch. I sent flowers to her at least once each week. We'd go to the movies, out to dinner at some of the nicer places in town or sometimes just to get pizza. We went on picnics in the park. It really didn't matter what we did, we were just having fun getting to know one another, during the week and throughout weekends.

You see, I found I hated eating without Paula. I hated going out to the movies without Paula. I hated traveling without Paula. Going to Gould, Pine Bluff, and just living in Danville without Paula was no fun. I'd discovered I was not especially happy anywhere without her. Our courtship lasted five years. Mind you, I asked Paula to marry me two weeks after we'd met, clear evidence of how quickly and completely she stole my heart. But, she'd just completed her first year of law school and understood that her studies needed to take precedence over our budding romance. After a full summer of dating, she confessed she loved me; but she also made clear her intention to complete law school. Indeed, Paula shared with me her goal of graduating, landing a job and living on her own for a while before getting married. I wasn't excited about that. I'd heard the old adage of "absence making the heart grow fonder, for somebody else." I didn't want to risk losing her due to distance. She attended law school at Case Western Reserve University in Cleveland, Ohio which was over four hundred miles from Danville. I was nine years older than Paula; I was thirty-two years old and she was twenty-three when we met. That made me a bit more ready to settle down than was she. She assured me that if we were meant to be, it would all work out. It took a while. But, eventually it did.

During the time we dated, we each took the time to learn one another. We spoke honestly about what we valued, what we wanted to accomplish, the places we wanted to visit, what we feared and how we wanted to live. I found that while we had grown up in different places and in differing family circumstances, we shared many things in common too. We'd both struggled through adversity and succeeded; our families were important to us and we each held them in high regard; we both valued education, were committed to saving the money we earned to reach goals; and most importantly, we both had an abiding faith in God. We had our differences too; but we committed to talking to one another and to working through them. The magnetic force I felt for her endured and she shared it.

The path was not always easy. We each had insecurities to overcome. But, we stuck to it and eventually the timing worked out. It took five years, but we committed to marry. We got married on May 31, 1986. Unita was Paula's Matron of Honor, Lolita was a bridesmaid and Johnnie, an accomplished songstress, sang Barbara Streisand's arrangement of "Evergreen" at our wedding. Paula included two of her first cousins, Carolyn and Anna-Marie, another dear friend from high school, Kimberly, and my youngest sister Levette as brides maids. Our wedding was both beautiful and memorable. Once joined, I was committed to making it last.

I'd learned from my first debacle that to stay married, one had to work at it. It wasn't just about *feeling* the love, it was more about making the *decision* to love even when you didn't feel like it. Indeed, it was especially then. Forgiveness is also a big part of being in a marital relationship. One needs to learn to forgive one's spouse no matter what they have done. And, that is *impossible* to do without Christ. Indeed, it is expressed best in scripture: "Though one may be overpowered, two can defend themselves. But, a cord of three strands is not easily broken." *Ecclesiastes 4:12* The most poignant lesson I learned was never to allow the word divorce to enter into the marital discourse. You see, I believe that if divorce is considered an option, chances are you will take it. Similar to playing football, rugby or any closely quartered contact sport, marriage can get ugly. So, one had best establish the rules of play up front. Paula and I made a pact that no matter what, divorce would not be an option. That agreement has caused us to work together on our issues as they come up before they fester. It helps us to remember why we are together and how much we love one another. Let's be real, we might not "like" one another all the time, but our true love remains.

That commitment has served us well. At this book's writing, Paula and I have celebrated thirty-three years of marriage. All glory goes to God for that blessing and joy. The second and most important thing that I've learned about marriage is that for it to work, Jesus Christ must be the head of the marriage. There are few things guaranteed, in life or in marriage, but having Him at the head provides the best chance to succeed.

Journey to Success Notes:

CHAPTER TEN

NEWLY MARRIED ~ MORE LIFE CHANGES

When we got married in 1986, Paula and I moved to Crawfordsville, Indiana. Crawfordsville, a small rural community, was half-way between Danville, Illinois and Indianapolis, Indiana. After graduating from Case Western Reserve University Law School in 1983, Paula was hired by Barnes & Thornburg, the largest and one of the most prestigious law firms in the State. She'd done well in law school, graduating near the very top of her class. She again broke racial barriers in her career. She was the first female African American Associate to join the law firm. I was hanging in there at General Motors, but with the challenges confronting the automotive industry, I was open to moving from the Central Foundry Division. She was doing well at the firm and had landed General Motors as one of her steady clients.

After we got engaged, one of the Vice Presidents she counseled at GM asked what she planned to do after the wedding. She confided that her husband wouldn't mind being considered for a transfer to one of the plants in Indianapolis. Because many of GM Plants were closing and things weren't necessarily coming up daisies in the automotive industry at the time, we knew it was a long shot. However, the Vice President said he'd do what he could, acknowledging that it might take a while to accomplish. We decided that Crawfordsville was as close to midway between Danville, Illinois and Indianapolis, Indiana as we could get and so we moved there.

The weekend Paula and I moved to Crawfordsville, the Ku Klux Klan (aka the infamous "KKK") held a march in downtown Crawfordsville. Paula and I laughingly retorted that they just wanted to welcome us to town. In truth, the march had been planned before our move, but it clearly showed us the sentiment of some of the people in town. Crawfordsville had a population of approximately sixteen thousand people with less than two percent African Americans. We couldn't understand why the Klan felt that they needed to march. To their credit, the city's citizens opposing the demonstration seemed to outnumber those present in support of the Klan. But it still gave us pause to see the willingness of some to put their bigotry on such open display.

We'd been in Crawfordsville about a week and hadn't seen anyone of color. Then one day as we were driving down the street, we saw a black man sitting on the side of the road next to a truck with a barbeque trailer attached to it. He was selling ribs and chicken. We were ecstatic to see him. Stopping quickly, we hopped out of the car and ran to meet him. His name was Mr. Norvell. He welcomed us to town, letting us know that he, his family and a small community of black folk had lived in town for many years. He invited us to his church the following Sunday; we immediately said yes.

Crawfordsville Home & Community Life

When Paula and I moved to Crawfordsville, we first lived in a small apartment just off Indianapolis Road. We spent parts of our weekends driving around looking at the various neighborhoods in town dreaming of a home in which we could settle and build our future. Learning from my past financial mistakes, we committed to maintaining discipline over our spending. We wanted a comfortable home and a lifestyle befitting of our hard work; but, we also wanted peace of mind. The psyche of the GM employees at the time, if they had any sense that is, held some fear and trepidation. Layoffs were frequent and one's financial obligations did not simply evaporate because the income disappeared for a time due to a reduction in force. Thus, determined to do what we could to avoid the pitfalls we'd seen others stumble into, we decided to make sure that we could pay all of our financial obligations from one of our incomes. That way, if the dreaded loss of a job for either of us occurred, we would be able to stay afloat. And, if we refrained from overspending, we would have a nice nest egg to help ward off fiscal insecurity.

Within a year, we'd saved enough money to make a sizable down payment on a home. We chose a house located about four miles outside of Crawfordsville on two acres of land. The house was situated out on State Road 47 North. It was beautiful; what we liked to call a diamond in the rough. It had a country feel to it and was about five years old when we bought it. The family we purchased the home from had somewhat flamboyant taste in terms of the colors and décor they appreciated. The front entry sported a bright green and yellow foil wallpaper; the carpeting in the formal living and dining rooms was the same boisterous green. The bedrooms, of which there were four, also had vivid and incongruous colors on the walls and floors. And the four bathrooms did too. But all the rooms in the house were spacious, and the floor plan had an inviting flow. The eat-in kitchen had two large picture windows that looked out over the generous rolling back lawn, and there was abundant farm acreage behind that, which we could see was planted with corn. Lucky for us, many potential buyers were put off by the loud color scheme. Paula saw opportunity. She loves to decorate.

Indeed, if she wasn't a lawyer, I'm confident she could make a good living as a professional interior designer. To her, the place was a blank canvas on which she later would display a masterpiece. The house had sat on the market for a bit as a result, and that was beneficial for our negotiations. We made a great bargain and were able to preserve a nice bit of our savings for our decorating budget.

Our next-door neighbors, who predictably were white, were initially quiet but friendly. We shared a mutual gravel driveway that split off into separate sections after about sixty feet or so to get to each of our respective houses. While the neighbors didn't host a formal welcoming party when we moved in, they spoke to us politely and we had no issues agreeing on things like sharing the cost of gravel for the upkeep of the driveway. They had two boys; one was the age of my son. When Sherman Louis would come to stay for the summer and for school breaks, he and the neighbor's sons played together and became very good friends. This opened a window for the adults to engage more often and genuinely to become friends.

As mentioned, our house sat on two acres of land. Behind us, there were about thirteen acres of farming land that ran behind four other neighbors' homes. A utility company wanted to buy the land to install a cellular phone tower. Our next-door neighbor found out about the plan and shared the information with us. We got all the neighbors together to attend the Zoning Committee Meeting of the City Council where the cellular phone company's proposal was being heard. We unanimously opposed the building of the tower in what amounted to our back yard. We gave testimony on why the tower was not desirable i.e., how it would lower our property values as well as being a nuisance to our neighborhood lessening our quiet and peaceful existence. The City Council stayed its ruling, indicating that they would give us thirty days to buy the land from the current owner. It was clear that if we didn't purchase the land, they would allow the cellular phone company to buy the land and build their tower.

The neighbors got together the following week at our home. Each agreed to purchase a portion of the land. Paula and I agreed to purchase four acres and the other three neighbors would each buy three acres. Paula drafted the purchase agreement, and the sale of the property was completed. The experience brought all of our neighbors closer together. Indeed, from that point on, we were not just neighbors but friends. It was a great experience for us all; a small group of citizens got together, challenged a big corporation and the city, and won. Needless to say, the real winner was the improved relationship that this established between us and our neighbors.

One aspect of life in Crawfordsville that struck us as odd after living in town for about a year was that we never ran into other African Americans in any of the restaurants or stores there. We would look, but never saw anyone. We speculated that there was an unwritten rule or custom that blacks weren't really welcome at the local restaurants or stores. We'd made it a practice to go out to dinner at the nice places in town on the weekends and, honestly, had never had any issues. But, we never saw any other people of color. We asked local black folk why they didn't go out for meals at any of the restaurants and were told that they preferred to go to Indianapolis whenever they went out for dinner and to shop for furniture and other things there as well. Still, it seemed odd. Indianapolis was nearly fifty miles away.

Within three weeks of moving to town, my wife and I accepted Mr. Novell's invitation and visited the Second Baptist Church. To say it was small is an understatement. An average of eight adults and six to eight children attended the church on any given Sunday. On our initial visit, the pastor immediately pursued us to become members. After attending for a few Sundays, we decided to join. Instantly, we were put into service in the church. I had been a deacon at a Baptist church in Danville; therefore, I was ordained a deacon at this church without delay. I was enlisted to become the adult Sunday school teacher; Paula taught the children's class. We both joined the choir, which was kind of funny because I don't even sing in the shower. When we joined the church, the choir was composed of four members. So, they clearly were happy to have a few additional warm bodies, which we provided.

I even was asked to fill in for the preacher when he went on vacation or needed to be absent for any reason. Pastor John Wells lived in Indianapolis. He and his wife, Louise, drove down each Sunday for church and on Wednesdays for the regular prayer meeting and bible study. He was an exceptionally devoted and humble man of God. When we joined the church, we learned that his salary was barely enough to pay for his gas to travel back and forth from Indianapolis. Shortly after our joining the church, we proposed, and the members agreed to give the Pastor a raise.

In addition to the aforementioned duties, we also provided transportation for the children that attended the church. There were kids from several single-family households, and they lived in poverty. Paula and I would pick them up, take them to church and provide them with breakfast every Sunday. As we noticed that their clothes and shoes were in need of replacement, we bought them new ones. My wife started bringing a comb and brush to church with her, often combing both the boys' and girls' hair. They didn't like that. She told them if they wanted to avoid it, they needed to take care of it themselves before we picked them up. Over time, we saw significant improvement in both their cleanliness, overall grooming and self-esteem. We held an annual summer party at our home for the church; the kids looked forward to it each year.

The church also had a relationship with a few students from Wabash College, an all-male college located in Crawfordsville. Paula and I frequently attended plays, talks and other activities at the college. Over time, we developed relationships with a number of the students. Remembering our own college days, we'd invite the students over for dinner on Sundays. A home-cooked meal is always a welcomed treat for a student. Years later, two of the students we came to know from Wabash College became employees of Eli Lilly and Company (where Paula and I both later were employed). Each did exceedingly well, one joined Lilly's law division and the other the marketing division. We maintain close relationships with them both to this day. During our time there, we became a part of the small African American community in Crawfordsville. The church and its members became the center of our lives there. We established life-long friendships that we maintain and cherish.

But, after six years living in Crawfordsville, Paula received an unexpected phone call from the Vice President of Human Resources at GM. He'd been her client when she worked at Barnes & Thornburg. A year after we married, Paula had left the prestigious firm to join Eli Lilly and Company as in-house counsel. The Vice President was over Human Resources at the General Motors Allison Engine Company plant in Indianapolis. Before Paula and I married, he'd indicated that he would work to get me transferred. As the years progressed and the transfer didn't happen, we simply moved on making the best of our situation. General Motors was going through a precarious time economically; many thousands of employees, both salaried and hourly, were being laid off or if they were lucky being moved from one plant to another. Salaried employees were finding moves increasingly difficult to obtain, especially moves maintaining one's salary classification. We'd maintained our relationship with the Vice President over those years, typically seeing he and his wife at social occasions and at least once a year at the Circle City Classic football game in Indianapolis. When we got the call asking if I was still interested in transferring to the Allison Engine plant, my immediate response was, "Yes!" I got my resume together, came in for an interview and things got moving quickly.

This was God at work. At the time, the Danville plant where I worked was in a state of tremendous flux. There were incessant rumors of a possible plant closure, but nothing had been formally announced. A few choice people had been transferred around the country to other GM plants. But, as a whole, the company was not allowing anyone to apply for a transfer. Only company-initiated transfers were permitted.

Shortly after I interviewed at the Allison Engine Division of GM, having returned to work I received a call to report to personnel. I was informed that Central Foundry, the division of GM where I worked, had been *instructed* to transfer me to the Allison Engine Division's plant in Indianapolis. The management team was perplexed. What I didn't yet realize was that the local management team had absolutely no input into my transfer. They were *told* when, not *asked* if, I would be transferred. Indeed, the move was scheduled to occur within a few weeks. When the word got out that I was being transferred to Indianapolis some of my colleagues were happy for me; and as one can imagine, others were envious.

Within nine months of my transfer, it was announced officially that the Danville Central Foundry Plant was closing. Not one Danville employee, salaried or hourly, was transferred to Indianapolis even though GM had at least three other plants there. Some employees were transferred to Michigan, Ohio, New York, Tennessee and many other places around the country. Without our friend's help, I would have never been transferred to Indianapolis.

When Paula and I shared the news that we were moving with our Crawfordsville church community, they were simultaneously devastated and pleased for us. They hosted a big celebration to commemorate our departure. While the local church was small, it had grown over the six years we'd been there and the church maintained "sister church" relationships with the Methodist Church in town as well as with other predominately African American churches in Lafayette, Green Castle, Terre Haute and Indianapolis. They invited the sister churches to the celebration, and it was very well attended. Virtually, every adult local church member spoke at the event expressing what we'd meant to the church, the children and the entire community. We were touched immensely by the love shown to us. We vowed to return for visits to the church's anniversaries and other milestone events at the church, and we have.

Selling The House In Crawfordsville

We got our Crawfordsville home ready to put on the market. We were concerned about selling the house. We'd lived on the country road for about six years at this point, and several of the homes on the road had been put on the market over that period. They'd typically taken a significant period of time to sell. Based on that history, we contemplated and were prepared for a delay in selling it. Because we'd become accustomed to the daily fifty-minute drive from Crawfordsville to Danville and to Indianapolis, we decided to be patient on selling the house and were willing to hold out until we were able to get the price we thought the house was worth.

We'd made positive improvements, inside and out, on the property. Paula had put her impressive decorating acumen to work inside. We replaced all of the carpeting, updated the wallpaper, put in custom draperies and had bought classic hard and soft furnishings that complimented the home. We believed the house would show well. We contacted a local real estate agent. She came out, walked through the house and proposed a realtor walk-through with a number of her colleagues. The vocalized "oohs and wows" were plentiful on that realtor's walk-through. She proposed a price she thought we should list the house for on the market. Paula and I listened, discussed it and decided we thought the house was worth more than the price she proposed. We instructed her to put it on the market for twenty-five percent more. The Open House was scheduled. However, the day before the Open House, the agent called to ask if we would be willing to show the home to a person that was in town that day but would be gone the next. We agreed. To our utter surprise and delight, the house sold before the Open House for our asking price!

We hadn't yet found a house in Indianapolis. We aggressively began the search. Because we'd agreed to a closing date with the buyers of our Crawfordsville home, we needed to quickly find a home to avoid a two-step move. We contacted a popular Century 21 agent and shared with him what we were looking for. Within days, he invited us to Indianapolis and showed us a number of houses. We soon realized that the market in and around Indianapolis was much more expensive than the Crawfordsville market. The agent was very pushy, trying to get us to buy a house more expensive than we wanted to buy. After a few days, we decided to let him go.

Brownsburg, Indiana ~ Why Not?

Brownsburg is the first little town to the west of Indianapolis on Interstate 74. And, thus, Paula would often stop at the gas station there on her way home from work. There was a quaint little shop that specialized in linens located at the strip mall next to the gas station. There she'd peruse the soft furnishings she'd fashion to beautify our home and to satisfy her retail therapy cravings. I had no complaints; Paula shopped smartly and could be depended on to get the finest quality at an astutely negotiated bargain. The gas station and little strip mall were our total exposure to Brownsburg.

Once my transfer was finalized and we'd sold our home in Crawfordsville, we needed to get moving on buying a new home. The agent we hired to help us pushed us toward homes in Carmel and Zionsville, the areas many professionals were drawn to because of the reputations the cities had for excellent schools. We weren't as concerned about the school systems, because we didn't have children to enroll. We liked the homes we were shown but weren't as impressed with the asking prices. After being drawn into a bidding war on one of the homes in Carmel we were interested in, Paula suggested we consider Brownsburg. Based on her limited exposure to the town, her impressions were positive.

We went to the real estate office located off State Road 231 and asked for their assistance. The agent was friendly and helpful. The homes we were taken to consider had a much more elegant feel than our Crawfordsville home. Don't get me wrong, we loved our home, but this was the next level. Our house in Crawfordsville had a rustic country ambiance, at least on the exterior. And, as was pretty typical for its age and period of construction, the ceilings in our house were only eight feet high. After visiting newly constructed homes, we felt claustrophobic upon returning to the Crawfordsville home. Cathedral-ceiling entries were now the norm. Many of the properties we saw also featured master bedroom suites with ornately decorated ceilings and many rooms were enhanced with detailed crown molding and ceilings and ceilings with a minimum height of ten feet throughout the rest of the house.

We soon found the perfect spot. It had all the bells and whistles we could have imagined; a dramatic entry, nice master suite with cathedral ceilings, and with skylights in the master bath over a spacious jacuzzi tub. It even had what would be our first walk-in closet. The place was situated as *the* capstone house at the very front of the two-year old subdivision. A meticulously maintained lawn set off the home's curb appeal. The owners hadn't spared expense on landscaping either. Both the front and back yards had plenty of well-positioned shrubs, flowers, decorative trees and tastefully designed pebbled pavement. The home was situated at the top of a small lake, and even had an in-ground swimming pool with crystal blue water. The view from the eat in kitchen was breathtaking.

We considered several other homes but returned again and again to the one in the Ironwood Lake subdivision. And, because the sellers were newly married and had just completed construction on another new home in town, they were motivated to sell. We negotiated a price forty thousand dollars less than our offer for the property we'd nearly purchased in Carmel. Needless to say, we were delighted.

The family that had purchased our home in Crawfordsville were natives of the town transferring back home after a brief career-driven hiatus. They too were anxious to close on the sale. We each awaited loan approval on our respective mortgages, but things were moving quickly. No looming issues appeared to be on the horizon. Because things were moving along so well, we ambitiously scheduled the closings on both houses to occur on the very same day.

Closing the Sale on the Crawfordsville Home

There was one small hiccup. Closing the sale on the Crawfordsville house was scheduled in the morning, and the Brownsburg closing was going to take place in the early afternoon. The day before the scheduled closings, we received a panicked call from our real estate agent relaying concerns expressed by the mortgagor for the Crawfordsville buyer. The expressed concern was that there was no formal easement running with the land on the shared driveway on the property. This was a surprise to us as it had not been an issue to the original owners of the house and had presented no problem when we purchased the home. But, the mortgage agent had firmly countered that unless an easement was agreed upon, executed, notarized and duly filed prior to closing, they would not approve the purchaser's loan.

We'd already agreed to purchase our new home in Brownsburg, and both of the closings were scheduled to occur the very next day. Paula and I contacted our next-door neighbors and explained our dilemma. They were as surprised as we were that this was an issue but agreed to do whatever we needed to get it resolved.

Luckily, Paula had experience in drawing up legal descriptions and easements from her work at Barnes & Thornburg. In retrospect, it was somewhat comical watching her out there with a huge tape measure surveying the gravel drive. We measured from the State Road to the start of the drive; the total width and proceeding depth of the shared portion along with the total distance of each driveway. We found the survey pins embedded in the property and measured the official distances from them to the shared drive. We set forth where the easement rested within each property and clearly outlined the provisions for shared maintenance that each land holder would adhere to.

Paula drafted the legal description, established the official terms and shared it with our neighbors. They agreed to the terms without change. We didn't have a printer at the house, but our neighbors did. So, they invited us over to complete the administrative tasks. Fortunately, one of our other neighbors was a notary public, so we were able to get that accomplished without fanfare. We got matters wrapped up around midnight. Paula rose early the next morning and got the easement filed at the Office of Titles & Deeds as soon as the office opened. We delivered the officially filed easement to the bank's mortgage loan officer that same morning. The sale of our Crawfordsville home was completed without a hitch. The positive relationships we'd built with our neighbors made it all possible. We thank God and them for that blessing. We maintain contact with them and their children to this day.

The Brownsburg Welcoming Committee

Two weeks later and three days before Christmas, we moved to our new home in Brownsburg. The move was handled as a part of my GM transfer so professional movers packed and unpacked our household goods. This enabled a smooth transition for us. The organizing and purging we did before the move paid huge dividends. We told the movers where we wanted the furniture and other home furnishings placed; they even unpacked the kitchen contents, neatly putting items in our pantry, clothing, linen and basement storage areas. They did virtually everything. Within days, everything was unpacked and settled. Paula's family even joined us for Christmas dinner.

Like us, many of our new neighbors were transplants to the city. United Airlines had constructed a maintenance hub at the Indianapolis airport. Hendricks County, where Brownsburg is located, was beneficiary of many of the employees that transferred into the State from across the country. Our initial reception was good. One neighbor welcomed us with a sugar cream pie; another family even invited us to join them for Christmas dinner. We didn't accept the invitation but did make arrangements to get together with them later in the new year.

Our initial impressions of the city were positive. However, within a span of two to three weeks, things started to change dramatically. We received a call from the real estate agent that had sold the house to us. Calling from the beauty parlor where she was getting her hair done, she worriedly reported that an unsavory group in town was threatening to burn a cross in our front yard. Well aware that the likely origins of such a group were none other than the Ku Klux Klan, Paula immediately asked what time the group planned on coming? She said we wanted to know so we could provide hot dogs for the wiener roast. The agent was in tears, her anxiety palatable. Paula asked that she simply relay our message.

Paula's counterintuitive response was grounded in the belief that the Klan's actions were always aimed at intimidation and designed to instill fear. We wouldn't grant them the privilege. Indiana has a long history with the Ku Klux Klan. A group grounded in and focused on white supremacy, the Klan appeared in the mid-1800's in American history. Its primary mission was to defend and maintain the white way of life, free of minority influence or progress. Its strong-armed tactics included the lynching, shooting, stabbing and whipping of anyone they considered to be operating outside the norms they desired to be maintained.

The Whitfields, it would seem, would have its own unique history with the Klan. I didn't have to dig too deeply in my own memory to recall the store owner in Gould that had boldly advertised the date and time of the next Klan meeting in his store window. Paula's family had its own experiences as well. Her father, an executive with Quaker Oats, accepted a position in Jackson, Tennessee in the early 1970's shortly after the public schools were integrated following a long court battle. He and his wife, Helen, courageously purchased a home in Holiday Gardens, an all-white neighborhood that adjoined the Country Club located just outside the Jackson city limits. Their initial reception was far from kind. But, they persevered with their five children and broke many racial barriers in the city.

And, I also recalled that a mere six years before, Paula and I had witnessed the Klan dressed proudly in white robes and hoods marching openly through the commercial streets of Crawfordsville. We couldn't help but think, "here we go again." It was 1992 in Brownsburg, Indiana, but the Klan was still alive and well. Next, we learned that the home our real estate agent had under construction was vandalized by fire making it clear that the local chapter of the Klan was indeed mobilized and seeking to terrorize us and anyone who had anything to do with supporting our move to the city. On more than one occasion, we awakened to see our garage doors and cars splattered with eggs. On several nights, we were treated to the loud, boisterous shouts of obscenities predictably using the "N" word telling us to get the hell out of Brownsburg. We called the local police; they responded promptly and made detailed reports of the incidents.

Needless to say, we were bothered and had serious concerns for our safety. But, honestly, while we couldn't help being irritated and understandably angered, we also had an abiding sense of peace in the situation. Our home wasn't equipped with a security system, so we added one immediately. We had a firearm that my father-in-law had given us when we moved to Crawfordsville. He'd then been concerned because I often worked the night shift and Paula was home alone. We'd never had to use it then, but in Brownsburg I kept it close by should the unfortunate need arise to protect my family.

Things calmed for a few days with no incidents. Then, a neighbor stopped by early in the morning. He introduced himself and, obviously embarrassed, showed us a sign that had been left in his yard. It was a big sign that said, "Ni##€rs," Get the ϴFuxκ Out of Brownsburg." (Note: the yard sign included the actual insulting and profane words). Sheepishly, he said he thought it may have been intended for us. Again, we notified the police.

The same neighbor came over a few days later to let us know that his children, students at the Brownsburg High School, had overheard some older students at the school plotting to make a bomb out of bleach and acid to place in our mailbox and under our sports utility vehicle. He said he wanted us to know, be on alert, and implored us to take precautions. He voiced his willingness to talk to the police and that he would let them speak to his children as well.

Next, our realtor called again to let us know that their office had received a threatening letter. The letter was one like you see in the movies, you know, where words are cut out of magazines and taped to a piece of paper. Not exactly high tech. The letter threatened to burn both the agent's house and to torch the real estate office for selling a house to "Ni##€rs." (Note: the yard sign included the actual insulting and profane words). She was fearful, both for us and her own family. She worried about what the Klan would do next.

Because Paula was knowledgeable of the law, she was intrigued that the Klan had chosen to use the U.S. Mail to relay its threat. Using that public utility, she said, made it a federal problem. We contacted the regional FBI office. The Klan had crossed the invisible line using the U.S. Post Office to spread fear and intimidation. This action brought civil rights and hate crime statutes into the picture. The FBI quickly came to speak with us about everything we had experienced. We shared with the authorities all of our experiences to that point. The agents said they would speak with the local police to get their reports.

A few days later, a local lawyer, and long time resident, Harlan Hinkle, stopped by our home and introduced himself. He said that he had heard we were having trouble. At this point, the problems we were experiencing were common knowledge in the small closely-knit community. Harlan apologized for the behavior being displayed and offered his help in resolving the problem. We shared with him all that had happened since we'd moved to the town. We expressed our surprise at how a city could be so close to Indianapolis and yet be so unwelcoming to us. As he intently listened, he rightly came to the conclusion that we had no idea that we were the first African Americans to move to Brownsburg. He interrupted our explanation of events and asked, "Do you all know that you are the first African Americans to move into this city?" We looked at each other with shock and disbelief.

We told him we knew that there were not *many* African Americans in Brownsburg, but we'd understood that there were *some* because when signing in at the local realtor's office; we'd seen pictures in the town brochure of two African American teens playing on the girls' basketball team for the high school. He looked at us and, with what we'd later come to recognize as the signature Harlan grin, confessed that the two had been adopted by a white family in town. They had since graduated high school, and the family no longer lived in the city. It all began to make sense. Harlan went on to share that he was happy we had moved to Brownsburg explaining that the town needed to progress, to move forward, to embrace change and grow into the place he knew it could be. He asked that we give the town some "undeserved patience." Harlan acknowledged the "bad apples" in town but said he didn't believe them to be representative of the entire community. Committing to help us in any way that he could, he invited us to join him at church the following Sunday.

We did a little research on Harlan Hinkle. As it turned out, he was one of the best known and highly respected lawyers in Hendricks County. He and his wife, Carole, had raised a family and lived in the community for decades. He owned property throughout the area and had a great deal of influence. We came to understand that Harlan knew virtually everyone of consequence, positive or negative, in the community. We learned that he was a man of action, not just words. And, that when he said something, his words could be trusted.

The following week we got a call from the city's mayor. He'd just gotten off the phone with the local television station in Indianapolis. Aware of the issues we'd experienced, the media wanted an interview. The mayor was very concerned about the bad publicity this could bring to his city. He introduced himself, and quickly made clear that he was well aware of the problems we were experiencing. He assured us that he was taking our issues very seriously and revealed that he'd had the chief of police assign officers on each shift to make special patrols of our home and to uncover the identities of the individuals responsible. Acknowledging that his city was far from diverse, he said that he and others were committed and working to change that. He related his fear that if word of our experience got out into the media, the little progress they'd made in the city could be set back years.

Imploring us to refrain from talking to the media or allowing reporters to bring their cameras to Brownsburg to give his city "another black eye" when it came to diversity, the mayor promised to get to the bottom of who was behind the problems. I told him that I appreciated his call and that I would discuss his request with my wife. I also let the mayor know that we hadn't moved to Brownsburg to start problems.

I was confident that the mayor was sincere. Paula and I had a long discussion on the pros and cons of involving the news media. Our primary concern was safety; the safety of ourselves and our beloved little Shih Tzu dog, Skippy. The pain and depravity that unleashed hatred could cause was not something we wanted to experience first-hand. We'd received several threats and we took them seriously.

To be clear, neither Paula or I were concerned with being "the first," or "the only," African Americans in town. That had been true for both of us for much of our lives. Being different wasn't a problem. Standing out wasn't a problem.

But, we weren't interested in putting our lives at risk. That said, we both had an intrinsic confidence and peace in the situation. We liked our new home and had good feelings about the community. We were not interested in allowing the bad elements to have success in running us out of town. Paula also shared that since we didn't know Brownsburg was an all-white town when we'd decided to move there, maybe God intended for us to come and help enact change. And, she shared if that was the case, God would take care of us. Born and raised on the south side of Chicago, Paula has always been fearless.

So, we agreed to stay. Within thirty minutes of our discussion, we received a call from the Indianapolis television station. The caller said that they were well aware of the threats and racial issues that we were having in Brownsburg and wanted to meet with us to get our story. We told them that we were fine and did not want to meet with them. They pushed back very hard persistingly explaining that it was important that people know how badly we had been treated so that no other African American would have to go through this in the future. We held to our position. They finally relented but asked us to contact them immediately if we changed our minds. We called the mayor and updated him on our decision. He thanked us and reassured us that he'd take care of the problem.

The FBI agents also got involved and did their work. They met with us and with our neighbors. Looking predictably professional and seriously competent, they visited the high school flashing their FBI identification badges. They interviewed several students both to learn what they knew, but also to let them and others in the community know that they were involved, ready willing and able to take action to protect us from the unsavory elements in the community.

Our home security system was completed with motion detectors and glass break detectors. Our master bedroom was located upstairs. The first night after its installation, our Shih Tzu Skippy set off the motion detector triggering the alarm. We'd barely gotten downstairs when we spotted the patrol lights flashing in our driveway. Turning off the alarm, we went to the door. The police officer, seeming more panicked than us, asked if everything was alright. Explaining that Skippy had set off the motion detector, we told him we were fine. He explained that he'd been patrolling our house regularly and that we could be confident in an immediate response if we had any trouble. The incident proved that the mayor was a man of his word. After that, we had no more issues.

Within a few weeks of moving to Brownsburg, Pastor Harold Leininger of Calvary United Methodist Church stopped by to welcome us to the city and invited us to his church. As it turned out, this was our second invitation as this was the same church that Harlan Hinkle attended. The following Sunday, Paula and I became the first African Americans to attend the Calvary United Methodist Church. Within a month, we were active members and serving on committees and teaching Sunday School.

Six months later, I received a call from the Chairman of the City Council asking if I would consider serving on the Police and Fire Board. I had no idea what the responsibilities were for the board. Paula explained that the community was reaching out and trying to be inclusive; that I was educated, intelligent and as able as anyone else to contribute to our community. The next day, I called back saying I would be pleased to serve on the board. I figured that this could be a win-win situation.

A month later, the Chairman of the Brownsburg Library Board called asking if I would consider serving on their board. I said, yes. We later learned that one normally was required to live in the city for two years before being asked to serve on such boards. Obviously, they waved that requirement for us. We also learned that Carole Hinkle, Harlan's wife, was instrumental in making it possible for me to serve on the boards.

The neighbors in our Ironwood Lake subdivision had always been amicable. But soon, others in the broader community started being noticeably friendly. People greeted us politely and by name as we shopped in local stores around town. They'd wave at us when we were out and about at restaurants and other social spots. In a small town one's profession and personal details are not too difficult to discern. They learned that Paula was a lawyer at Eli Lilly and Company and that I was in management at Allison Engine Company. Our professional pedigrees shouldn't have mattered. Others seeking to move into the city were not subjected to such a litmus test. But, it gave them comfort and smoothed their transition and acceptance of a bit more diversity in their town.

They came to understand that we were no threat to the community and simply wanted to live our lives in peace. We went from being called the "N" word to being referred to as the Huxtables from the then popular Cosby television show. When my son came to spend summers with us, the neighborhood kids made him feel welcomed. They'd come over to ask him to play, and he'd spend the entire summer building friendships and just having fun. The neighborhood children also spent many afternoons in our backyard and pool. Another illustration of the heart of the immediate community we learned to love came in the spring of our first year there. One of the neighbors bought two ducks; one white and the other black and put them in the lake behind our home. The ducks became a symbol of friendship, acceptance and hope. If ducks could live together in peace and harmony, perhaps we could too.

Brownsburg was our home and became one of the best cities that we'd lived in. We made authentically true friends in

Brownsburg who remain to this day. Within three years or so, another African American family moved into a subdivision on the other end of town; and the next year still another family moved into the city. At the time of this book's writing, Brownsburg's African American population is over five hundred which amounts to nearly two and a half percent of the city's population. We are proud to have made a small contribution to the progress of that fine community.

Journey to Success Notes:

CHAPTER ELEVEN

MY NEW ROLE AT ALLISON ENGINE COMPANY

The General Motors plant I transferred to was Allison Engine Company, a Division of GM ("Allison"). Allison made jet engines for the C130 aircraft and helicopter engines for the Osprey helicopter. When I accepted the new position, I wasn't sure of the job I would hold. Being assured that I would maintain my management level was enough for me. The plant in Danville was closing and many of my co-workers and friends wouldn't be as fortunate. I counted myself extremely blessed.

Upon arrival for my first day of work, I was introduced to the Head of the Quality Department. He had interviewed me before they'd submitted the paperwork for my transfer. But, on this day, he informed me that I would be in his organization. I would hold the position of Senior Quality System Auditor. My job was to perform audits of the quality systems of outside vendors and part suppliers. This was a new job for me, but my previous responsibilities in manufacturing had taught me the importance of quality in being able to deliver a marketable product.

I was introduced to the quality team and assigned to shadow each member for a two-week rotation providing me the opportunity to learn what each of their jobs entailed.

Following that, I went out on several road trips to observe exactly how an audit was performed within a supplier's site. It didn't take long for me to realize that I liked this job much better than my old job at Central Foundry. The plant's work environment was far cleaner, and the work of hourly employees was more technical than at my previous plant site. After twenty-two years, I could finally wear a suit and tie to work. This had been my dream since childhood. I was delighted to work in a clean office environment and to both dress the part and be viewed as a professional. This job also was different in that I was an individual contributor. At Central Foundry, I had managed hundreds of people and had done so successfully. But, at Allison, I soon learned that I liked being responsible for doing my own work and that I got a greater sense of satisfaction from managing my own performance. I didn't miss having the people management piece as a part of my responsibilities.

Allison was still a Union plant, and it had all of the rules that I was very familiar with from my time in Danville. The big difference was that in my new position I wasn't involved in managing the hourly employees or the Union. I didn't miss it one bit. In my new job, I was required to travel throughout the United States. I visited vendors and suppliers of parts used to make our jet and helicopter engines and audited their quality systems. I was responsible for between ten to fifteen vendors, and my audits were based on the ISO 9000 quality system. If a vendor or supplier did not fulfill requirements, their parts would not be acceptable and wouldn't be used in production. Mine was a powerful position, and I took it seriously. I received significant respect from those I audited. They understood completely the ramifications should they not meet our quality standards. One errant screw or bolt in an engine could spell disaster for a pilot, his crew or innocent bystanders. Actual lives depended on our engineering a quality product. Our overarching objective and goal was to do all we could to make a safe and quality engine. I worked to ensure that our vendors and suppliers knew what was required and if they fell short in any way, that they made the corrections necessary to fulfill the quality standards.

After I was in the role for a year, a new requirement was introduced to the quality team. Each of us had to pass an exam given by an external certifying organization to stay in the auditor's role. The exam had a seventy percent fail rate for those taking the exam for the first time. Passing was mandatory, so the pressure was on. We were given a manual to study that included every process involved in auditing a quality system. There was immense pressure to pass the exam on the first try. The team members were given three months to study and take the exam.

At each staff meeting, the Department Head would announce who had passed the exam, which also made clear who hadn't. I studied hard. My evenings and weekends were consumed with studying the materials in preparation for the exam. The Study Manual had sample questions at the end of each section. I reached the point where I could confidently answer every sample question.

Exam day came. It was on a Saturday. Two exams were administered on the same day, the Engineering Technical Auditor Exam and the Quality Systems Auditor Exam. I was confident. Indeed, I felt a little over prepared because I didn't want to experience the humiliation of failure. There were thirty or so of us from different companies that sat for the three-hour exam. I received the exam from the proctor and moved through the questions in half the time allotted. I then took my time going over the questions and my answers again before submitting my completed exam to the proctor. I left the testing center confident that I'd done well.

Results were promised in thirty days. Both anxious and excited, I waited. My results arrived in the mail on a Saturday. I had heard from others that if you passed, you would receive a manila envelope with your official certificate of completion. I opened the mailbox, and there was a regular letter-sized communication, *not* a manila envelope. My heart seized and dropped before I even opened the letter. I knew this was not good news.

Paula, well aware of my expectations, was just as impatient in awaiting my exam results. She'd witnessed how hard I had studied and had diligently helped me take the practice tests. So, when I was reluctant to open the letter, she opened it and read it to me. Not only had I failed the exam, the letter revealed that I had answered over fifty percent of the questions wrong. I was shocked. Confounded. Devastated. Sickened that I would have to report my failure to my boss and co-workers.

That same day, we'd planned to visit Paula's family in Chicago. This was close to a three-hour drive from Brownsburg. On the way there and on the drive back home, we lamented over how after so much preparation I could have done so poorly on the exam. I resolved that the Lord didn't want me to pass the exam; that maybe he was punishing me for something. Perhaps I'd been overly confident, my attitude too assured, strident, cocky. Paula didn't buy it. She focused instead on the low pass rate and said I simply needed to refocus my efforts and try again. I still couldn't believe that I done so poorly.

We returned home on Sunday and having mustered the courage to read it again for myself, I retrieved the letter. I read it and hollered. Yes, the letter informed me that I had failed the Engineering Technical Auditor Exam. But, I hadn't taken *that* exam. I'd taken the Quality Systems Auditor Exam. They had used the wrong answer key to score my test. With renewed hope, I showed the letter to Paula. She said, "Wow, God does answer prayer." She hadn't detected the discrepancy because she didn't know two different exams were given at the same time at the testing location.

Neither of us got much sleep that night. First thing Monday morning, I made a call to the examiners and related my concerns. They committed to look into it and to get back to me right away. Within two hours, which seemed like two years, they called and confirmed that I was right. They were almost as excited as I was. They had run my exam using the wrong answer key. Instead of failing the exam, I had aced it! They promised to correct their records and immediately mail my positive results and the official certificate evidencing my success to my home.

I was overjoyed, but I also was humbled. Paula and I breathed a collected sign of relief, and then we celebrated. I didn't say a word to anyone at work until I received the official certificate in the mail. I brought it in to work and presented it to my boss. He made a copy and put it into my personnel file. A total of eight auditors took the exam. Four additional auditors passed eventually; of the eight, three others took it several times and never passed. My experience helped me empathize completely with those that didn't pass the exam. Of course, I was happy that I had passed. But I didn't consider myself superior to those that didn't. My experience made it abundantly clear that but for God's grace, I could easily have been one of them. And I knew, firsthand, how that would feel.

I enjoyed my job at Allison Engine thoroughly. I traveled about forty percent of the time going from the east to west and the north to the south coasts of the country. My travel schedule was mine to make, so I never felt flustered or over-wrought. Responsible for writing the audit reports and sharing my findings with the suppliers, I generally provided my findings to those audited before I left their plant. If there was disagreement, we could discuss it before I left the facility. Once back in the office, I'd provide a copy to my management. Within a week of the audit, I sent a formal copy to the supplier. They were given from between thirty to sixty days to submit corrections to my audit findings. The suppliers I audited routinely took auditors out to dinner. Some would even offer to do "other things" that were not permitted. They were surprised that the GM auditors would not accept their offers of lavish dinners, golf or other inappropriate entertainment offerings.

I considered it of the utmost importance that I establish a professional relationship with my suppliers and part of doing that was establishing my integrity with them. If we had lunch or dinner, I paid my own way. If they offered other things, I respectfully declined. They quickly learned that I meant business and that I respected them for the work they did for us. Nothing more, or less, was required.

Two years into my new job, GM decided to sell the plant to a management group that included senior members of the current plant's leadership. One of the requirements of the new owners was that all salaried employees had to stay with the plant and could not transfer to another GM plant. This meant that all of our GM benefits, including the GM profit sharing, 401K, healthcare and retirement pension benefits would no longer be in effect. One good thing was preserved; our GM retirement benefits were frozen and, thus, we would be entitled to receive a pension and other healthcare benefits from GM once we retired. The new owners provided employees with an opportunity to participate in a new 401K plan. After the sale, everyone had a new seniority date; the same date the plant was sold.

The UAW employees were not affected by the sale of the plant. They could choose to transfer to another GM plant or stay with Allison Engine Company. Whichever choice they made; they would receive the same benefits as before the plant was sold. This irritated the salaried workforce because we were not being treated as fairly as the hourly workforce. We were at the mercy of the new leadership. This was a clear case where the Union power was leveraged to protect its members ensuring that they were treated more positively than management.

Those previously in GM's management had no recourse; they had no place to air their grievances. Some did file a lawsuit, but nothing came of it. Two years after the Allison Engine Plant was sold to the management group, it was sold again. This time, to Rolls Royce's Aerospace Division, at a huge profit. Again, the Union members were taken care of and didn't suffer changes to their benefits or pay. The salaried workforce, however, was powerless to do anything but to accept its new reality.

Hired by Lilly ~ A New Beginning ~ Faring Well

Within four months of Allison Engine Company's purchase by Rolls Royce, Paula was asked to consider a promotion and move to London, England. She had been in-house counsel for Eli Lilly and Company ("Lilly") for ten years and had done well there. She'd joined Lilly a year after we married and had quickly moved up the management ladder in Lilly's Law Division. At this point in time, she managed the team of lawyers and paralegals that handled legal matters for Lilly's global medical and regulatory organizations. She was offered what amounted to a double promotion; she would be General Counsel for Lilly's Europe, Middle Eastern and African operations. It was a big jump in responsibility that held significant prestige. She would be the first African American to hold that position, and the first woman in that job. Full of joy and excitement, she came home to share the news. In her work with Lilly, Paula had traveled extensively to many places in North America, Europe, Asia, the Middle-East, and South America. And together, we had gone on several vacations that helped us to appreciate the beauty and diversity of places outside our beloved Indiana.

Therefore, we weren't anxious about the possibility of moving to Europe for a time. When the position was offered, we were told the assignment would be between three and five years in duration. She'd turned down several opportunities of promotion before because of concerns for my career at GM. This time, we discussed the offer and the opportunity for future career advancement that it could mean for Paula. We also contemplated the timing of the offer considering Allison Engine Company's recent sale to Rolls Royce. My GM retirement pension and retirement healthcare benefits were frozen and, thus, protected. And, my tenure at Rolls Royce was minimal; so, while I was gainfully employed, I wouldn't be walking away from a great deal.

We surmised that this could be advantageous for Paula's career. But, we also understood that at forty-nine years of age I still needed and wanted to work. Our first thought was to approach Rolls Royce to see if we could arrange a transfer. As luck would have it, the corporate headquarters for Rolls Royce was located in England.

I approached Human Resources and explained our situation. My friend in HR, the same Vice President that had gotten me transferred to Allison, agreed to contact Rolls Royce to explore interest in my request. Rolls Royce Headquarters agreed to interview me for a position (similar to the one I held in Indianapolis) but indicated they weren't willing to pay for the trip. Paula discussed it with her management. To my surprise, Lilly agreed to sponsor my trip to interview with Rolls Royce.

Within two weeks, I was on a plane flying business class headed for Bristol, England. I spent a full day being interviewed by various members of management at the plant site. To be honest, they seemed more interested in the Allison Engine plant than my skills. Many of their questions related to the workforce and the work environment of the plant. But, my interviews went very well. Not only was I offered a position, they offered me a promotion. HR explained that they were thrilled to have someone from the newly acquired plant to help with its integration with their plant operations in Bristol.

I was pleased to be offered a job, and a promotion to boot. But once on the ground, I was concerned about the distance of the Bristol plant from London. When I shared the good news about the interview and job offer with Paula, we took a closer look at the map. Bristol was one hundred eighteen miles from where her office in London was located. That meant we'd likely have to live in Reading, a city pretty equally distanced between the two cities. Admittedly, this was kind of old hat for us. We had done the commuting thing when we'd married and moved to Crawfordsville, Indiana and lived between Indianapolis and Danville, Illinois. But, this distance would entail traveling either by train or by car on unfamiliar and far more congested roadways.

After serious reflection, we decided this wouldn't work. We went back to the drawing board. Paula explained the quandary to Lilly's General Counsel Rebecca Kendall. She went by the name Becky. She, in turn, asked Paula to bring my resume in for Lilly to take a look. Becky opined that Lilly had manufacturing operations in the United Kingdom ("U.K.") as well; perhaps we could make this work. We knew Becky well. Paula had worked for her for years. And, we'd socialized often and held one another in mutual high regard. A week later, I interviewed in Indianapolis with the head of manufacturing and engineering. During her tenure at Lilly, in one of her many assignments, Paula had been legal counsel to the head of Lilly's Engineering Operations, and we'd built a good professional relationship with he and his wife. He was also a fellow Brownsburg resident. This reaffirms the importance of building relationships; one never knows when connections can make a difference in a person's life. Choosing to build a bridge as opposed to burning it down can often make the difference between getting a job or not getting it. A kind word of support, a productively nurtured affiliation, or simply choosing to reflect a helpful demeanor can spell the difference between success or failure.

The next week, Lilly flew me back to the U.K. for an interview at Lilly's manufacturing plant in Basingstoke, England. Since I had over twenty-four years of manufacturing experience, I was hopeful there might be an opportunity for me to work there. But again, it was an all-expense paid trip for me. Paula accompanied me on the journey. She arranged to meet with some of the people that she would be working with in London should things work out.

The Lilly interviews were more challenging than those at Rolls Royce. While I had twenty-four years manufacturing experience, the manufacturing of medicine is very different from the manufacturing car parts and jet engines. However, at the end of the day, I was offered a position at the Basingstoke site. The precise job I would hold hadn't been fully defined, but we had a tentative agreement on my salary and job level. On those two important points, I was pleased. I told them that I would share the specifics with Paula and get back with them directly.

Excited with the developments, I shared them with Paula. Analytical by nature and true to form, Paula had a few questions: Was I going to be a U.K. hire or a Corporate hire? Was my Salary Scale based on the U.K. market or the U.S. market? Was I going to be an International Service Employee ("ISE") with said benefits? I asked her what difference did it make? She explained that if I was a U.K. hire, I wouldn't have a job when her assignment concluded and we moved back to Indianapolis; that my thoughts on salary were based on the automotive industry, not the pharmaceutical industry and there was a big difference between the two; that ISE benefits included a great many things including tax equalization benefits, car allowances, vacation benefits, to mention a few. I hadn't considered any of these matters, and I didn't even know there was such a thing as being a local hire versus a corporate hire. Thank God, Paula knew to ask the right questions.

I explained my concerns to the personnel director at Basingstoke and asked if I could be a corporate hire. He was reluctant indicating that he had no authority to hire corporately. I wasn't willing to accept a job in Basingstoke and be out of a job when we move back to Indianapolis. The next day, Paula and I met the Vice President of Human Resources for the Regional Operations in London. He explained that they were anxious to make the announcement of her promotion. As was typical and customary, the "daisy chain," caused by such personnel moves impacted many individuals that would be moving from one responsibility to another. Paula's proposed move would impact a significant number of others across several regions for the company i.e., a Country Manager in Austria moving from Europe to the Intercontinental Region, a move for the current General Counsel for Europe, Middle East and Africa to Austria; a move for the person slotted to replace Paula in her current position, and others further down the daisy chain. As opposed to being pressured, Paula said that Lilly needed to resolve *my* employment issue before *any* announcement could be made.

She knew that once she accepted the new assignment, any leverage she had would be lost, and all her negotiating power in getting Lilly to resolve my issues would evaporate. She held firm and told them that if I wasn't happy, the move wouldn't happen. We returned to the U.S., and Paula shared with Becky that the interviews had gone well and that she was willing to accept the new position *if* I was a corporate hire, not a U.K. hire, and *if* we came to terms on my salary, the timing of my eligibility for contingent compensation bonus, job level, and ISE status.

Within the span of a few days, all issues were resolved. Each of the demands Paula made on my behalf were accepted in my favor. I was a Corporate Lilly hire on an International Service Employee package with a salary and other benefits that I heretofore had not dreamed possible. Things could not have landed better.

Paula demonstrated by her actions how much she cared that I was happy with the move to London. She didn't exert one iota of pressure on me to accept the Basingstoke job. Indeed, she was willing to turn down an opportunity that represented tremendous advancement for her if I wasn't fully satisfied. She needed for me to be happy and convinced that it was a good move for me. After we got all the details ironed out and I got my formal offer of employment, she smiled and told me that the decision for her was simple. She said, "I haven't lost anything in Europe and don't plan to. I can get another job, but I cannot get another you." Gratified and humbled, I had no doubt that this was a move blessed by God. Now we could progress on a new journey that truly would impact the rest of our lives. We weren't sure what the future would hold, but we knew we would face it together with unqualified joy.

Journey to Success Notes:

CHAPTER TWELVE

MOVING TO LONDON

The first step was to get the Brownsburg house ready to sell. Lilly made that part easy for us. They had a corporate relocation company that laid out pretty simply all we needed to do. That was the positive thing about an international company move. They provided check lists for everything outlining step-by-step instructions on how we should organize our assets and other belongings to make things easier on ourselves as we transitioned to our new location. We could sell our home ourselves, or the company would buy it from us and resell it. Either way, we were guaranteed to get the market price. It took us about two weeks to get the house on the market. The same was true for our vehicles. We could sell them ourselves, or they would buy them from us. In either event, we were guaranteed the market price. We set our minds to selling two of our vehicles and to getting ourselves and our household goods organized. We sold our car to a neighbor, and our SUV to Paula's brother Bruce in California. We decided to keep my 1982 Corvette. To be honest, I was really attached to it and couldn't bear the thought of a stranger having it. Paula's brother Steven who lived in Green Bay, Wisconsin agreed to keep it in storage for us for the duration of our adventure abroad.

We next had to decide what to donate, pitch, sell, store or move with us. Lilly paid for storage of things we decided we couldn't part with but didn't think we would need in London. But, understanding that we would be gone for between three to five years, we knew we should keep that to a minimum. If we didn't really need it in Europe, we determined we likely wouldn't want it when we got back home. The company was gracious; we were not limited on the amount of furniture we could take with us. Still, the living accommodations we would have in London would need to be taken into account. We also learned that the 110-voltage used for appliances and electronics in the United States wouldn't work. The United Kingdom, and all of Europe for that matter, used 220-voltage. This meant that we either had to buy new appliances there or use electrical transformers for any electronics or appliances that we wanted to take with us. We decided to sell or give away all the small stuff i.e., coffee pots, toasters, can openers, vacuum cleaners and we invested in dual voltage television sets that could be used both in the U.S. and in Europe. We maintained our Lilly Credit Union bank accounts and other investment accounts, but we knew that we'd have to open new bank and credit accounts in London once we got there.

Lilly worked on updating our passports and on getting work visas for us, not an especially easy feat in the United Kingdom. We both took physicals and filled enough prescription medication to last at least sixty days until we could establish new primary care physicians in London. We had multiple farewell parties, given by family and friends from work and church. The whole process was simultaneously exciting and emotionally and physically draining. There were so many things to be done; and it was a far more complicated and different process than moving from one home to another within the States. But, we survived the preparations for the move.

Within two months, the house was sold. Our belongings were tossed, sold, given to family and friends, donated to charity, stored or prepared for shipment. It was an immensely heartrending experience to leave much loved family and friends. Yet, we knew that the Lord had his hand on our steps and was intimately involved in the changes in our lives. We were excited, but still there were so many unknowns to learn about actually living in a foreign country.

I reflected upon the bad experiences we'd encountered when we first moved to Brownsburg, and on the many positive changes that had occurred for us since then. We'd made true friendships. Calvary United Methodist Church, a significant part of our lives there, hosted a big farewell celebration for us and many of our neighbors were in attendance. We'd lived there for five years and had established roots. We were preparing to move to London to form new connections that hopefully would bolster our futures and help us develop even brighter horizons. While sad to leave family, our Brownsburg home and all of the close friends that we had made there, we knew happy times awaited us in a new place and we were excited to experience them.

Getting Settled

In August of 1997, we started our new lives in London, England, the land of afternoon teas, Christmas pudding, and a pub on every corner. It was a year full of transitions for us. We'd found 'a flat,' an apartment in American English, that was located within walking distance of Lilly's Regional offices located at the Lilly House on Hanover Square. My work assignment was at the Basingstoke Manufacturing Plant. It took me an hour and a half by train or an hour by car to get to Basingstoke. I'll give you one guess on who found the flat!

Seriously though, we wanted to live in London, a virtual beehive and treasure trove of activity in England.

Our flat was in Harley House on Marylebone Road located in the prestigious NW1 Post Code. We lived next door to the Royal Academy of Music and right across the street from the London Clinic, and a block away from the Madame Tussaud's Museum. Literally, our backyard was Regents Park, one of the most beautiful parks in London where the Royal Rose Garden is planted. Harley Street, the street Paula usually used in making her way to the office, is the street where many high-end physicians have established their practices in London for centuries. Our absolutely stunning flat was situated in the perfect spot. What we didn't have in square footage, in comparison to our Brownsburg home, was made up for in its elegant curb appeal, convenience to fabulous shopping in London's West End, the ease of transportation and our easy access to "green space," all highly coveted attributes in any big city.

We were provided living accommodations typically reserved for the rich and famous. Thirty-three Harley House on Marylebone Road had three large reception rooms complete with three fireplaces, a powder room, four bedrooms, four in-suite bathrooms, a laundry room outfitted with a washer and dryer, and an eat-in kitchen with built-in luxury appliances. The building was mansion block typed, fully gated, equipped with electronic security systems, iron gates and uniformed porters who manned the area twenty-four hours a day, seven days a week, providing personalized service to Harley House residents. We also were provided secured parking on site, something worth its weight in gold in London.

We started to work immediately upon our arrival. And, there was a lot to get used to. We had to establish bank accounts, get new credit cards, find new primary care doctors and learn the best places to shop for food, clothing and furniture. We even needed to learn the brands of household goods we should purchase. For example, at home we'd purchased Tide laundry detergent, Dawn dishwashing liquid and Crest toothpaste, but those brands weren't available in stores in London. We learned, both by asking our neighbors and by trial and error, what we considered to be good quality products in England. Purell was a good laundry detergent; Fairy Liquid was what most people bought to wash their dishes and Boots Toothpaste was what most folks used to brush their teeth.

We learned how the city's "tube" or metro subway train system worked, having made the decision to hold off on getting a car. We learned by observation how to drive with the steering wheel on the right side of the car and how to drive on the left side of the road. Figuring out how to maneuver in roundabouts, which went in the opposite direction of the ones we have in America, was more than a notion! Getting general utilities connected like a telephone, cable television and simple mail delivery proved more difficult than one would expect. We were told we might have to wait a while before we could get the cable connected for the television. The lines would need to be run and that required us being put on a production schedule, because only so many new lines were permitted in a given building.

We initially believed that customer service wasn't a priority for the Brits. After a year living in London, we came to understand that it was more us than it was them. We were in a perpetual rush to get everything done and demonstrated little patience, if any, when things didn't happen on the schedule we wanted. By way of example, when we went out to dinner, we were quickly exasperated at the long waiting times for a table. Indeed, we were perplexed at the responses of some restaurant hostesses early in an evening that they were "fully booked." When we sat down to eat, we were quick to call over a server to place our order. We ate expeditiously and were perturbed when we'd always have to waive the server over to get our check. We thought we were being polite, that they were rude and that we were being ignored. After all, didn't they need our table for other customers? Once we opened our eyes, we learned that the London custom was different. When we sat down at a table in a restaurant they expected us to be there for the entire evening. The tempo and pace of service, indeed, the entire dining experience was far more relaxed and hospitable. We needed to learn how to sit back, take a breath, relax and enjoy the entire experience.

Paula hit the ground running with her new job as General Counsel of Europe, Middle East and Africa. She needed to learn the new people, both her new business partners, her legal staff and the vast new territory within her responsibility. But she was still at the same company and was still practicing law. So, while it was a big transition for her, it was less daunting because she knew the players and had an established reputation at the company.

Conversely, I had to adjust to a new company, industry, job, foreign culture and work environment where I knew no one, except Paula; and she wasn't at my plant site. More importantly, I needed to establish my own brand and reputation. My experiences at General Motors and Rolls Royce could take me but so far in the pharmaceutical industry. And, the first few months would be important in that transition. First impressions are difficult to remake. And, I wanted to do well.

My first task was to figure out which train to catch that would take me from London to Basingstoke. Luckily, the Bakerloo Line (London Underground "Tube" or subway) was located directly across the street from Harley House. I took the Bakerloo Line directly to Waterloo Station and from there boarded the train to Basingstoke. The trip took ninety minutes one way. Once I got accustomed to the schedule, it was pretty simple and predictable. But little things like unfamiliar accents often could complicate what should be a simple journey. Because of my initial difficulty understanding British accents, I had trouble understanding many of the announcements, both over the loudspeakers at the station and once I got on a train.

I remember one morning running late, dashing through the huge and cavernous Waterloo Station and hopping onto the train. As the train pulled from the station, I breathlessly asked a fellow traveler: "Is this train going to Basingstoke?," just as the train started chugging down the track. Luckily, I was on the right train. On another day when traveling on the train from work, I thought I'd heard the announcement that they were "changing the crew." Because I was the only person sitting in the coach and the train sat unmoving on the tracks for what I thought was longer than typical, I got off the train expecting that another announcement would be made when the new crew arrived. The train took off down the tracks before I could get back on. I later learned that the announcement was that the passengers could change to a new line at "Crew," another train station stop. I didn't make that mistake again.

I soon became an expert traveler. Meaning, I knew where to line up to get the best seats on the train and even how to take a nap while riding the train and not sleep past my planned station of exit.

After we'd been there for about a year, one of the other Senior Executives working in London with Paula transferred back home to Corporate Headquarters in the United States. He had a Jaguar S Type luxury sedan. While both Paula and I were entitled to a car on arrival, we'd decided to wait to give ourselves time to adjust before trying to drive in the U.K. We liked his car, so Paula arranged to take over his lease. Paula walked to work, so she didn't need the car. But, we now had a car and I could drive to Basingstoke instead of taking the train.

Driving in London

Now that we had a car, I needed to figure out the best route to take to Basingstoke. It was 1998, before Bluetooth and satellite directed GPS systems were available in cars. Roads in England were designed before cars were invented, so the streets are extraordinarily narrow, winding and many are circuitous. Not only did I have to get use to driving on the left side of the road, I also needed to accustom myself to driving sitting on the right side of the car, where passengers sit in America. For me, this was no easy task. But, it was a matter of life and death for both me and fellow motorists should I mistakenly find myself driving on the wrong side of the road.

Another issue was the roundabouts. How does one enter and exit a roundabout? Not easily. In the U.S., most roundabouts have at most two lanes of traffic. In Europe, where roundabouts have been in use for much longer, they are larger with many more lanes of traffic entering and exiting simultaneously. This was especially problematic for me. Because I was blind on my right side, seeing oncoming cars revolving the traffic circle at a pretty-fast clip was unnerving. But, after getting yelled at and having horns blown insistently at me on several occasions, I soon figured it out.

I am thankful I never had an accident driving in England. At the time, the requirement was that expats needed to get a driver's license after residing in the country for one year. Passing the driver's test was challenging, even for Brits. The study book was the size of an unabridged Webster's dictionary, and it contained many more questions and driving scenarios than one could easily master. The Better Safer Motorists (BSM) manual contained over a thousand potential questions. Even if you studied hard, one always feared there would be totally different questions with different scenarios on the actual test. On the actual road test, you are graded not only on whether you signaled correctly, drove the right speed or could park the car with relative ease; they also considered whether you placed your hands on the steering wheel correctly, did you have your seat close enough to the steering wheel, did you stop at the railway crossing long enough to ensure that no train was coming, etc. Any misstep could cause you to fail the test. Most *do* fail on the first attempt. But, once one passed, people held big parties with friends and neighbors to celebrate.

First Day ~ Basingstoke

On my initial day of work, I experienced the feeling of a warm embrace. The people at the Basingstoke site welcomed me with open arms. Often during my tenure there, I was told I had a beautiful American accent. Never before had I considered myself as having an "American" accent; southern yes, American not so much. But, on reflection, it is what we Americans say about others from other countries. He has an "Italian," "French," "Spanish," or "English" accent, never thinking of how we must sound to them. Perhaps our views of ourselves and where we stand in the world needs further consideration. Maybe, just maybe, we're not the center of the universe. Perhaps we *all* have a lot to learn. But, on my first day at Basingstoke, people said they just liked hearing me talk; and that was a nice first day.

One notable difference working in the U.K. as an International Service Employee ("ISE") was that I was entitled to four weeks of vacation. When I started at GM, I was immediately entitled to a week. In my view, that was real progress. My first assignment was to an ad hoc team called Project World Class. The team was made up of twenty people from many different functional areas on the site. It was composed of "high potential" employees believed to have a promising future in leadership at the company. Individuals came from manufacturing, quality, finance, engineering, human resources, etc. Our primary objective was to look for ways to improve processes, procedures and to eliminate inefficiencies in all areas on the plant site. The goal was to make changes that would make Lilly's operations "world class."

This was an excellent place for me to start. It gave me the opportunity to learn about the different departments, the people and just how things functioned at the site. In the first two weeks, I was assigned to spend time shadowing different members on the team. Each would share what their jobs were and how their jobs fit into the overall functioning of the site. Interestingly, I found each person to be very interested in me. They'd ask, "Why are you here? How did you get this job? How long do you estimate you are going to be at Basingstoke?" They were quintessentially British and very polite. While it wasn't like they were drilling me with questions, it was abundantly clear that they were curious to know everything about me. Where were we living in London? Did we bring our own furniture from home or were we renting furniture? Did we have children? Where did I go to school? How about my wife, how long had she worked for Lilly?

When they took me to lunch in the cafeteria, I was the focus of attention. Not only was I the only American on site, I was a big, tall black guy which made me easy to pick out in a crowd. At that time, there were three other people of color at the site and they were from Ghana. This was my first experience working in such a demographic. It wasn't a problem for me. Indeed in my life, I'd never been treated so well. Interestingly, I wasn't referred to as "African American" or "black." I was referred to as the "American." Ninety-nine percent of the workforce was white, mostly Brits. But there also were a smattering of people from France, Belgium, Switzerland, the Netherland, Ireland, Germany and from other countries outside Europe. After two weeks of meeting people and learning my way around the plant, I was assigned to work with the team that had the responsibility of improving manufacturing process tickets.

My First English Friend

A teammate of Indian heritage named Martin Lale quickly became my closest associate in Basingstoke. A citizen of the U.K., Martin was born in England. His wife, Gurby, was born in India, immigrating to England when she was six years old. They both have extended family that still live in India. Within my first two weeks at the site, Martin invited me for dinner at his home which was located in Reading, England. He'd learned from our conversations that Paula often traveled during the week. Because of the distance of Reading from London, he invited me to spend the night.

Reading is located about thirty minutes from the Basingstoke plant site. Somewhat surprised by his invitation, honestly, I was reluctant to accept it. Martin, however, was insistent. He said he wanted me to meet his family. Martin and his wife Gurby had two young sons. He invited me to have dinner with them and to spend the night. He explained that we could leave Basingstoke, ride to his home and then come back for work the next day. Following this plan, I wouldn't need to worry about traversing the unfamiliar English roads at night. Paula was going to Germany the following week making it a good time to take Martin up on his invitation.

I packed a change of clothes. A multitude of questions permeated my mind. I'd known Martin for a very short time and, to be transparent, I had never known a person of Indian heritage. What would the food be like? What would the atmosphere be in his home? How should I interact with his wife and family? I'd made the commitment to go, and to spending the night. I prayed about it and that was that.

The following day, we got into his car and headed to Reading. On the way there, we made small talk. I questioned Martin about his family. He talked about his boys and their interest in of all things, football. We arrived at his home, a red brick house with a lovely backyard which they referred to a garden. Knowing now what I didn't know then, his home was impressively large for a middle-class home in England. Based on American standards, or at least the mid-western parts where space is not at such a premium, it would have been considered modest. The Lale home was exceptionally neat, soundly constructed and one experienced a warm welcoming spirit immediately upon entry. There were four bedrooms, several bathrooms, a large reception room, a dining room and a spacious kitchen.

On arrival, we were greeted by Martin's wife, Gurby, and their two boys. After a time, Gurby went to the kitchen to prepare dinner and Martin took me to the guest room to get settled in for the evening. Looking around his home, I soon grasped that I could have been in a home anywhere in America. I immediately felt welcomed.

After thirty minutes or so, dinner was served. Dinner consisted of traditional Indian foods, chicken curry, rice, samosa, creamed spinach with cheese, nan bread and a delicious dessert of ice cream. Gurby and Martin graciously informed me that it was quite okay if I didn't like something, that I could just push it aside. That wasn't an issue, everything was wonderful. I'd heard that Indian food is a hallmark of England, and I learned in my first meal with the Lale's why that is the case. It is an explosion of flavor. It was my first authentic Indian meal, and it would not be my last!

Our dinner conversation was friendly and comfortable. Gurby shared her first memories of arriving at England's Heathrow airport getting off the plane and walking through the snow in sandals. It was the first time she'd ever seen snow. Our dinner time conversation consisted of the usual talk about Paula and I, how long we'd been married, how I'd joined Lilly, where I had worked before that. I also asked them about where they had met and about how and when they'd married. That started a really interesting discussion on the Indian culture. They shared that their marriage had been arranged. It was agreed upon by their parents and, while they'd trusted their parents to keep their best interest in mind, they'd had nothing to do with it. While this sounded strange to me, I soon understood that this was customary in their culture and in their religious faith. The Lales were seits; a faith about which I knew very little at that point in my life.

The evening was relaxing. And, I felt very welcomed and comfortable in their home. In the morning, Gurby prepared a traditional English breakfast for us, which consisted of fried eggs, rancher bacon, baked beans, tomatoes and toast. Martin and I ate and left for work. The whole experience was awesome. As I look back on it, on being invited to a co-worker's home for dinner and to spend the night after knowing me for less than a month, it is just amazing. Martin opened his home and his family to me. Both he and his family opened their hearts and culture to me. I learned so much in the span of a day. It just goes to show what can be accomplished if people simply open their hearts and minds. If we are willing to accept the lesson, it is there for us to acquire and absorb. Nothing but openness and willingness is required.

Basingstoke Life

My initial job in Project World Class involved investigating how we could improve the manufacturing processes at the plant. We needed to understand where errors, inefficiencies and bottlenecks occurred so we could find ways to eliminate them. To gain understanding, I needed to get out in the manufacturing areas of the plant, interact with the employees, and solicit their inputs. As is often the case, those actually involved in doing the work are best positioned to know the problems and uncover potential solutions to them. So, I needed to speak directly to the employees on the manufacturing lines to discern the changes they wanted to see made to the manufacturing process documents. However, my experience at GM taught me that I first needed to gain a rapport with the employees. Without it, communications wouldn't be honest or meaningful.

I initiated a bit of a charm initiative to get the process started. I started by hanging out in the break area having coffee with employees. I'd walk around the cafeteria and ask if I could join groups sitting together. In my initial conversations, I sought to fit into whatever they were talking about. I asked about their families, bantered about football and connected with them on discussions *they* wanted to talk about. I soon realized that football (soccer in the U.S.), and the teams they supported, were the closest thing to God or the proverbial Holy Grail. It didn't take long. Soon employees on the shop floor would see me in the cafeteria or walking around the plant, and they would initiate the conversation. When passing in the halls, I'd give them a high five.

Our team was scheduled to provide monthly updates to the senior leadership in manufacturing on the progress we'd made on our assignment. Because Project World Class was considered to be a training ground for the "high potentials" on site, each member of the team was expected to give a formal presentation before the site's leadership at some point. After three months on the team, it was my turn. An agenda was provided prior to the meeting laying out what would be discussed and who would be on first base for the presentations. There was great anticipation on how the "American" would do. I had been present during other lead team meetings where updates had occurred. To engage the audience, I decided to get them involved in my presentation utilizing questions that tested their understanding of the manufacturing process and that revealed both the complexity of the process and the areas where simplification could improve efficiencies and benefit productivity. My finish was an impassioned plea for support of the team's recommendations to improve the manufacturing ticket.

The leadership laughed often and was entertained. More importantly, they were educated and learned a great deal. The feedback I received was very positive. Also, I was told that while they had heard Americans speak, they'd not heard one speak like me. I think it may have been the combination of southern drawl, Baptist fire and brimstone with a dash of street-smart manufacturing acumen that threw them off. I developed a reputation for being an excellent speaker. I was affectionately referred to as "The Shermanator," a name coined by Martin. Others began asking, "Have you been Shermanized yet?" Said in jest, I internalized and understood it as a great compliment.

I remained on this ad hoc team for six months. When we gave our final recommendations to the full site leadership team, our findings were accepted in full. The manufacturing process tickets were changed to reflect our findings. We also presented the findings and proposed changes to the employees making it clear that their inputs had played a huge part in the improvements that were to be made. Being on the project was a superb way for me to begin to learn the English culture, pharmaceutical industry generally, and the operations of the site. Most importantly, I got the chance to get to know the people and for them to get to know me. That had the most lasting impact on me. I learned that we all want the same things; to be heard, to be respected and to have the chance to make a difference.

With the successful conclusion of our project, it was now time for me to move into a real job. There were three options on the table. Because of my prior years in manufacturing, the first option was a role in manufacturing. The second was a position in the quality department reflective of my prior experience as a quality auditor at Allison. The third was a role in procurement where I would be responsible for purchasing raw materials used to manufacture and package drug products. Procurement had an immediate opening so that is where I was assigned.

I had never worked in procurement before and had zero experience with the raw materials or packaging products that I would be responsible for purchasing. But, I understood the importance of quality materials and the need to have unwavering confidence in one's suppliers. This was especially important when making medicines for humans and animals dependent on the safety and efficacy of drugs taken with the goal of helping, not hurting, them. The implications of including ingredients used to make medicines that didn't meet the highest of quality standards was unthinkable. I was assigned to work with a colleague experienced in procurement. I spent the first month sitting next to him learning how he went about the process of purchasing raw materials and packaging. A big part of the job was meeting with the external suppliers from whom we were buying the raw materials and packaging. Significant time was also spent negotiating prices for the products and services. This was a challenging time for me. I had to learn a great deal in a short period of time.

The person training me was scheduled to go on a week's vacation thirty days after we'd begun my training. I worked hard to learn as much as I could as quickly as I could in that first month. This meant I came in early and stayed late reading materials and learning the products. The month flew by in what seemed to me more like ten days. But, my time was up. I took over the job the following Monday.

Immediately, I started receiving panicked calls from manufacturing saying that they were running out of raw material and asking when the next shipment was due to arrive. I checked the schedule in the system, determined the delivery timing and got back with the manufacturing supervisor. He needed the product sooner than it was scheduled to arrive. I didn't know what to do. I immediately reached out to my supervisor. Phil Cooke had a reputation of being smart, detail focused and keenly knowledgeable of just about anything he put his mind to. He exhibited a no-nonsense approach to problem solving. If you needed to know something, he was your guy, you could be confident in his direction.

I explained the shortage issue I faced. He directed me to talk with another buyer in the group and to ask him to assist me in solving the problem. I did, and I was shown how to expedite a shipment of product. I had other issues in my first solo week. Each time I would go to Phil, and he would re-direct me to one of my colleagues to help resolve the matter. Without fail, they were willing to help and even admonished me not to bother Phil if I had an issue but to instead come directly to them. I followed that practice and it really sped up my learning curve. I soon learned and appreciated what my boss and colleagues were modeling for me; indeed, how most work was accomplished at Lilly. The relationships one built were the keys to success. Work was accomplished with the building of internal alliances and through the building of consensus. This was much different than how I had worked at

GM, Allison or Rolls Royce, where the management styles were much more prescriptive and "top down" in style. At Lilly, one was given much more autonomy; the result being that one felt more accountability and responsibility for achieving results.

The following Monday when my coach returned from vacation, another buyer went on a scheduled vacation and I filled in for him. He was responsible for buying different raw materials, but the process was the same. By the end of my second solo week, I had a pretty good handle on how to purchase material; but, I was yet to meet with a supplier or sit in on a price negotiation. The third week on the job, I was given the lists of the raw and packaging materials for which I was responsible. My responsibilities included the purchasing of materials and the negotiation of new prices when each of the contracts expired. Of course, the understood goal was for new prices to be lower than the previously contracted price.

I sat in on a few pricing negotiations before my first independent negotiation was to take place. Six months in, I was feeling comfortable in my procurement role. I was in the job for a year before my first pricing agreement was up for re-negotiation. I'd learned that the price paid was influenced predominately by the volume of each order. And, after further discussion with my supplier, I discovered that it took the supplier longer to set their machines up than it took them to run our orders because their machines ran so fast. The supplier explained that they had to set up and breakdown their machines each time they produced one of our orders. They did this weekly, sometimes four times a month. Considering this, I asked a simple question, "Why don't you run a month's worth of product in one set up?" They responded that they would love to do that; but the problem was if Lilly sent a change in requirements, they'd be stuck with the excess product made in the run. I asked how often we made changes, and I was told it occurred rarely. They acknowledged Lilly provided plenty of notice unless the change was an emergency change, which again was very rare. Contemplating this, I asked, "How much of a price reduction would Lilly receive if we agreed you could produce a month's worth of our product in one run and warehouse that product at your site ready to be shipped on demand?" Their response, "Sherman, we would give Lilly the biggest price reduction ever and would cut your lead time by sixty percent." Instead of having multiple set ups to produce the product when the supplier received an order, the product would be ready and sitting in the warehouse ready for shipment. The supplier then asked if in the rare instance that there was an emergency change in specifications, could Lilly agree to split the cost of the obsolete product? He admitted that he'd never had a conversation like this with any buyer from Lilly. I asked my supplier to write up the proposed agreement based on our conversation and send it to me so that I could have a discussion with my leadership and get their buy-in. He agreed. Within a week, I had the proposed agreement. The draft outlined the proposed change in lead times and a huge price reduction based on Lilly allowing them to produce ahead and hold our product in their warehouse.

I reviewed the agreement with my boss. After many questions for understanding and astute challenge, he agreed that we should try out the new process. It worked very well, and we booked significant cost savings. It became the new standard with all suppliers where the process made sense based on the product.

I developed great relationships with my suppliers because I treated them not simply as suppliers but as partners. I learned from my interactions that my way of dealing was somewhat contrary to the way suppliers were treated in the industry. But, it paid huge dividends for me and for Lilly. I excelled in my role in procurement. After three years, I was promoted to the next level which meant I now had the same job level as my Basingstoke boss. Needless to say, this was not well received by some of my colleagues. They attributed it to me being an American. That wasn't all together untrue. Because I was a corporate hire, my salary classification was tied to comparable jobs in the U.S., and my progress was being watched from Corporate Headquarters. That explanation, while accurate, didn't make it any easier for me with the locals.

When I called Mother Dear to tell her about my promotion, she asked for specifics about my job in England. Jokingly, I told her that I was buying and selling drugs. She didn't get the joke. I explained more fully that I was working for Eli Lilly and Company, a company that made pharmaceutical drugs; that I really was buying the raw materials necessary to make legal medicines. She said, "Okay boy, but don't scare me like that again."

Once my quality system auditing skills became known, auditing responsibilities were added to my procurement job, and I was added to the vendor auditing team. A team of us would schedule an audit of a supplier. This was a job with responsibilities similar to those I'd held at Allison and Rolls Royce. We'd travel to the supplier site, spend a few days auditing their quality system, prepare a report based on our observations and review the findings with the supplier while on site. We'd then give them between thirty to forty-five days to correct any deficiencies.

Our suppliers weren't just in England. We purchased product across the region. So, we audited companies in Germany, Italy, Spain, France, Belgium the Netherlands and many other locales. I got to interact with people of many different nationalities and to experience many cultures in the process. This provided a tremendous boost to my understanding of the world. I wasn't in "Kansas" anymore and man o' man, that was a good, fun and awe-inspiring thing. But just like in the Wizard of Oz, I came to realize that what I needed I'd had within me the whole time.

Church Life

Paula and I visited many churches in and around London. Our requirements were simple. We wanted to join a congregation where Jesus Christ was the main focus of the message and teachings of the church. We visited some churches that locals would refer to as the "high church" of England. At such churches, one got the feeling you were attending services in a Roman Catholic church before Vatican II. The Mass, the main part of the service, was at a big alter and was recited in Latin with the minister's back turned to the congregation, similar to how it had been done in the Roman Catholic Church until the mid-1960's. These churches proved a bit too formal and ritualistic for us.

We decided to join a church located within walking distance of our Harley House flat called All Souls Church. It was a congregation of the Episcopal Church of England which meant it was considered both catholic (with a small "c," meaning universal church) and protestant. The Queen is Head of the Church of England, a position that all British monarchs have held since it was founded by Henry VIII in the 1530's. The Queen appoints archbishops and bishops on the advice of the Prime Minister. The spiritual leader of the Church of England is the Archbishop of Canterbury. We did a little research on the Church of England, a portion of which is listed here:

<u>*THE CANONS OF THE CHURCH OF ENGLAND*</u>

Two of the important articles listed in the Canons:

A 1 of the Church of England:

The Church of England, established according to the laws of this realm under the Queen's Majesty, belongs to the true and apostolic Church of Christ; and, as our duty to the said Church of England requires, we do constitute and ordain that no member thereof shall be at liberty to maintain or hold the contrary.
A 5 of the doctrine of the Church of England:
The doctrine of the Church of England is grounded in the Holy Scriptures, and in such teachings of the ancient Fathers and Councils of the Church as are agreeable to the said Scriptures. In particular such doctrine is to be found in the Thirty-nine Articles of Religion, The Book of Common Prayer, and the Ordinal.

Many expats from around the world who were working in London attended. The congregation was made up of people from more than forty countries and was very active in providing food and other service to the homeless. It wasn't unusual for us to see homeless people sleeping around the perimeter of the church during the week, but they would all leave before church services on Sunday morning. The message delivered on Sunday morning was the message of Jesus Christ. Clergy didn't water down the message to accommodate the more than forty different nationalities attending the church. On any given Sunday, many in attendance were tourists visiting London because the church was located just a few blocks from Oxford Street. Oxford Street is one of the busiest shopping areas in London. We quickly joined a bible study fellowship group which proved to be one of our most fulfilling experiences during our time in London.

The fellowship group was hosted by Marion and James Barrett. Their home became our home away from home, and its members became and remain our London-based family. The group met bi-weekly and proved to be a cohesive United Nations of sorts. The Barretts had hosted the group for many years. James was an aerospace executive and of English heritage. Marion was German but had lived in England for many years. In addition to being extremely hospitable, kind and having keen and in-depth bible knowledge in the five years we attended the bi-weekly meeting in their home, we never recall having the same dinner or dessert twice. Marion was a superb cook and had the spiritual gift of hospitality. At various points in time, our bible study fellowship group was made up citizens from England, Scotland, Ghana, Ireland, Poland, Hungary, New Zealand, Germany, Austria, and of course America. The folks came from all walks of life; there were professors, diplomats, computer engineers, small business owners, fellow expats, and even a long-time secretary to the Queen. We came together to study God's word and built what proved to be lasting friendships with fellow travelers. Indeed, we are God parents to the child of one of the couples we met in the Bible Study group. Roy and Liz Shiromani, and their son Sam, have proven to be especially dear and precious to us.

On occasion, I was asked to read the scripture during the morning worship service at All Souls Church and was told that I read with the passion of Billy Graham. Each Sunday worship service included a prayer for the health and welfare of the Queen. The one thing I found strange was that even though the congregation was diverse and representative of many nations, the vicar, or pastor in U.S. parlance, and associate pastors, numbering three to five at any given time, were all white men. The ministers may have come from

Ireland, Scotland, Wales, Canada, Australia, New Zealand or any number of other countries affiliated with the Church of England, but during our time there not one was female or a person of color represented in the clergy.

But, we loved attending All Souls Church, and they made it clear to us that they loved us back. Those days will forever hold a precious place in our memories and hearts. Indeed, the relationships that we formed are just as strong today as they were when we lived in London. This proved to be true several years after we'd returned to the U.S. While at All Souls Church, we developed an especially close relationship with Rico Tice, an evangelistic minister at the church. While we truly loved them all, Rico was our favorite minister there. He was an athletic and stockily built Scot who loved rugby and playing sports. His sermons were always biblically based, pointed and full of life in delivery. We made a true connection in our time there in church and out, socializing after Sunday services and meeting up on occasion for dinner or at the local pub. Our friendship continued after we made it back to the States. Several years after returning to the States, Bruce, one of Paula's younger brothers died tragically. It was devastating. It was pure unadulterated hell for her and the entire Taylor family. Rico called Paula regularly to check on her. He sent books on grieving and often called her, in what for him would be, the middle of the night. He proved to be far more than a pastor to us; he was a perceptive, thoughtful, ever-present and consummate friend.

Paula and I have visited London at least eight times in the last nineteen years. Without fail, we manage to meet with members of our group for services at All Souls. After church, we share a meal at one of our favorite local restaurants, either our Turkish favorite Sofra or Pizza Express, both located a mere stone's throw of the church. And, whenever possible, we worked in an attendance at the bible study group.

After two years at Basingstoke, I started an on-site bible study. When we started, there were only three of us in attendance. Once word got around, the number increased with regular attendees growing to between seven and eight people. Two members of senior management attended regularly; one would even teach the class on occasion.

One Christmas, we decided to sing Christmas carols during lunch on site. I would walk the line as colleagues waited to place orders for lunch and asked if they knew Jesus Christ. My colleagues would say with joy, "Sherman only you would have the nerve to do that; and secondly, only you could get away with it."

Though Brits are not known for evangelism, the bible study proved to be a safe environment for them to share and embrace their faith. Two years after I joined the procurement team, my friend Martin joined the same team. We would have lunch almost daily, and I started to witness to him about Jesus Christ. He would share his Sikh faith with me. I learned that sikhism, or sikh, meant "disciple," "seeker," or "learner," and is a religion that originated in the Punjab region in the northern part of India around the end of the 15th century. In the Sikh faith, there are ten gurus. The first was Guru Nanak who lived from 1469-1539; the last Guru, Gobin Singh, lived from 1666 to 1708. It is the fifth largest religion on earth. Seventy-five percent of the approximately twenty-four million sikhs live in the Punjab region of India. We had many respectful and passionate conversations about our respective faiths.

After six months or so, Martin agreed to attend the bible study that I was hosting. He attended the studies regularly but maintained doubts, still holding fast to his Sikh faith. I convinced him, after about two years, to attend a course called Christianity Explored that was hosted at our church in London. It was run by Rico Tice, our favorite minister at All Souls Church. The course was designed to look plainly and simply at the beliefs of Christianity. It was a six-week course held from six o'clock to eight o'clock on Wednesdays and, it included a meal. Because London was some distance from his Reading home, I explained that he could ride to London with me and stay with Paula and I on the evenings the classes were held, and we'd ride back to work together the next morning. I assured him that the course was non-threatening, and no pressure was put on anyone to join the church or accept Christianity.

Martin agreed to come, but he didn't commit to attending the full six weeks. He came to the first session, second and third; each time I wondered if he'd come the next week. He did. At the end of the sixth week, he accepted Jesus Christ as his Lord and Savior and became a Christian.

Based on our discussions, it was clear that it would be difficult for him to tell his wife or any of his family that he had become a Christian. His father was a leader in his local Sikh community. I understood his predicament. Making this decision could negatively impact his relationships with his family, friends and social community. I assured him that he was under no pressure to share his faith until he felt comfortable with doing so, if ever. My friend continued to come to bible study, and he and I even went on a weekend retreat with All Souls Church. He continued to grow in his faith, and, after a time, his reluctance diminished, and he did share his faith with his family.

Meeting the Queen of England

Another highlight of our time overseas was meeting Queen Elizabeth and her husband Prince Philip, the Duke of Edinburgh. Paula, along with the other American senior executives of major corporations, received an invitation to attend a reception hosted by the American Embassy. Spouses were included in the invitation, which increased my expectations immensely. The reception was to be held at Winfield House, the official residence of the United States Ambassador to England. Winfield House is a mansion in Regent's Park, one of London's most impressive parks, located right behind our flat in Harley House. We often passed Winfield House on our frequent strolls through Regents Park. It is an expansive residence sitting on an estate of twelve acres and has the second largest private garden, topped only by Buckingham Palace, in the British capital.

The reception was grand, as one would expect. Scrumptious hors d'oeuvres, cheeses, canopies and sweets accompanied by wine and spirits were served. Before Her Majesty and Prince Philip arrived, we were advised on how we should conduct ourselves during the visit e.g., we were not to approach the Queen. If she wished, she would extend her hand. If, and only if, she did so, we could shake it. Thank goodness, we were told that there was no need to bow or curtsey. One clearly needed formal instructions and practice to do that!

When the Queen arrived with her entourage, everyone was very excited. My impression was that she was welcoming and friendly to all in attendance. She had a wonderful smile. Queen Elizabeth was positioned before the line of people who waited with excitement to meet her. She greeted us with a smile and made polite conversation with each individual presented to her. I was one of them. Her safety and security were of utmost concern, so no impromptu approaches or uninvited movements were permitted. That said, there were plenty of smiles and respectful nodding of heads in the room.

Meeting the Queen at a private event was a once-in-a-lifetime event for us. When considering that fewer than one percent of the United Kingdom's citizens ever attend a private event with the Queen, we felt pretty darn special indeed. There I was, a cotton picker from Gould, Arkansas, meeting the Queen of England. This was something I never imagined could happen. It was something special. Yes, the Queen is a human being, and in God's eyes no more special than me. And, I firmly believe in the old saying, "I am no better than anyone, and no one is any better than me." But in the grand scheme of things, this private reception with the Queen *was* special. And, it reinforced in me that one should never limit the trajectory of one's life. Impressive, remarkable, extraordinary and astounding things can happen when you least expect them. Imagine a life absent of boundaries, free of constraint. We must remain open, be hopeful and ready to experience the good things life has to offer when they occur. Hold fast to hope, for a good measure of joy can be just around the bend.

Ascot

We spent three of our five years' time in England in London. During that time, Lilly lost a big patent lawsuit involving Prozac, its blockbuster anti-depressant drug. The loss was unexpected and meant billions of dollars of loss revenue for the company. A sharp cost-cutting period ensued. One of the belt-tightening changes involved the closing of Lilly House, the regional headquarters for both Lilly's European and Inter-Continental Operations that resided in London at Hanover Square. The decision was made to integrate Lilly's western and eastern European regional operations with its research and development site at Erlwood Manor in Windlesham, a small town in the County of Surrey, England. Erlwood Manor was located about fifty miles from London. The Inter-Continental Operations, which encompassed Lilly's marketing and sales operations for everything other than the United States and Europe, were relocated to Indianapolis. This was a big move. Lilly House had been the center of Lilly's European and Inter-Continental operations for many years. It was the true hub of all sales and marketing activities outside of the United States and served as the global host location for many activities. But, the loss of the Prozac patent was real. It was profoundly consequential for Lilly. Much of Paula's work involved travel across both western and eastern Europe and beyond, but her permanent office space was now fifty miles from our flat in London. She now had to travel by either car or train to her new office.

She tried the train for a week. That wasn't good because her days started earlier and ended later than mine. She was arriving home late and returning to work early. We decided she should try driving. Now she was driving, facing all of the traffic and roundabouts, and witnessing the unkind drivers' disapproving gestures evidencing what they *really* thought of her driving skills. After one week, she phoned me from the car, stuck in London's traffic, both exhausted and frustrated and asked me to call the real estate agent. We needed a place nearer to her Erlwood office in Surrey. Ever the obedient husband, I reached out to the company's real estate agent. The following weekend, we started looking. Luckily for us both, moving out of London would put me closer to Basingstoke as well.

We'd become accustomed to flat living during our time there, but we couldn't find anything close to what we had in London. We found the area to be much more residential home focused. So, we started looking at homes as opposed to flats. We considered homes in Windsor, Earley, Maidenhead, Eaton and Sunningdale.

We ended up settling on a lovely estate in Ascot. It was called Orchard House, on Priory Road. The two-story brick home was one hundred seventy years old and sat on an acre of land with two stone patios. It had a red-brick nine-foot tall walled entry with an electronic security gate. The home had a spacious eat-in kitchen with the largest central island we'd ever seen, five bedrooms, five bathrooms, a huge formal living room, formal dining room, sunroom, separate library, and spacious storage and laundry room. Each room in the house had its own working fireplace. And, while the house was one hundred seventy years old, it had been beautifully renovated maintaining the original hardwood flooring in the dining room, sunroom and library. We even had our very own detached two-car garage. The home was absolutely stunning. What made it even more impressive was that the asking rental price on the home was significantly less than what we'd paid in London for the flat.

And, the estate's location was phenomenal. Orchard House was located on a quiet road a mere mile and a half from the famous Ascot racing track. In our time in England, Paula and I, with our Lilly expat friends, attended the Ascot horse race at least once each year. While there, we enjoyed the thirst-quenching drink called a "Pimms," a mixture of lemony soda or ginger ale, fruit, cucumbers, mint and a shot of fortifying gin. The Queen's Mum (Queen Elizabeth's mother) who was still alive when we lived there also frequented the races and was known to enjoy a nice Pimms' Cup; it's also served at the Kentucky Derby.

Now settled in our new home in Ascot, and once Lilly provided us with a second automobile, both Paula and I were happy with our respective commuting times to work. The only downside was that we had to travel back to London for church and to attend our bible study fellowship group. We learned more about the social life and activities outside of London and were happy to have the opportunity to experience both London and a bit of the "country life" of England as we sojourned there. The easy access to the London theatres, shopping, hair salons, and exotic cuisine was gone. But, we soon learned that England's Berkshire and Surrey counties had loads of culture to offer as well. The winding roads, country inns and nearness to a multitude of historic landmarks were close at hand; we learned to love this part of our journey as well.

A Taste of "White Privilege"

Paula and I lived in England for five years; each exhilarating, thought-provoking and unique in its own way. As an African American man, I'd never felt as accepted *as a person* in my life. When I say I felt accepted, I don't mean that I felt accepted as an *African American man*. I mean, I felt accepted as a man, a person, a human being. Period. I felt like I was "seen," "accepted," and "appreciated" for the first time.

But, it wasn't only in England. We felt the same in many of the places we traveled to across Europe. We visited Paris often during our time there. One evening while there, Paula and I had planned to go out for dinner. We'd made reservations but couldn't find the restaurant. I spotted a woman that happened to be getting money out of an automated teller machine. The ATM was located directly on the street outside the bank, as most are in Europe. I walked over to the woman and asked if she knew the restaurant we were searching for. She replied, speaking English with a lovely French lilt, "Yes, let me just finish getting my money please." When she'd finished, she grabbed me by the arm, led me to the corner and pointed the way to the restaurant.

As Paula and I walked to the restaurant, she said, "Do you realize what you just did?" I absently replied, "What?" She said, "You walked up to a white woman at night, at a money machine, and asked her for directions to a restaurant." Surprised at myself, I said, "Wow, I didn't even think about it." We had been living abroad for just over a year, and I'd gotten so comfortable being treated like a "regular" person that I had forgotten. I'd begun to act just like any other person, not like an African American man. In the U.S., I never, in my wildest dreams, would have considered walking up to a white person, male or female, at night at a money machine to ask for directions. This experience provided an infinitesimal glimpse of how the world could be if we stopped judging one another based on one silly criteria, pigmentation. Flesh, bone, blood and, skin, the largest organ of the body, infused with a thing called melanin, holds such power over us in our world. But, for some stupid reason, it seems to make all the difference. Pigmentation is the determinant of how so many make decisions on how they consciously and unconsciously value and treat one another. But, it doesn't have to be that way.

This was just one example, but a very poignant one, on how living in London and traveling across Europe impacted my views on life and our place in it. Honestly, I felt my color no longer caused me to be treated differently. I'm not saying that there was no prejudice, not by a long shot. There was inequality based on class in Europe. We saw plenty of that and understood that it could be insidious as well. But for us, the fact that we were Americans living where we lived, staying at the places we stayed, eating in the restaurants we chose, and visiting the places we toured seemed to go the extra mile. People were invariably respectful and kind to us. We've traveled on six of the seven continents on earth, and what we've felt on each was a sense *and* spirit of welcome.

What amazed us also was that there were many black folks in London. Loads of people from Africa or from principalities previously colonized by Britain lived in London. But Paula and I were never mistaken for another nationality. In all our travels, no one ever mistakenly thought that we were from Africa or anywhere else but the _good old_ U.S.A. Indeed, if we got on an elevator, or were just standing in line to buy theater tickets or were at the check-out line in a store, people would ask "what part of the States are you from" before we'd even spoken a word. A cynic might say our American arrogance seeped through, which might be true in part.

To us, it seemed instinctual, a foregone conclusion to them that we were American. This amazed us; so much so that Paula eventually asked Elaine Pugh, her administrative assistant, what the deal was. How was it that people in London, indeed, all over the world could tell that we were from America. Elaine laughed and said that it was easy. When in an elevator, in London anyway, only an American would look at others and acknowledge their presence. She told us, "Brits mind our own business." In addition, she explained, "Your teeth are straighter, whiter *and* you still have most of them. Moreover, you all tend to look people directly in the eye." These characteristics are not common in other nationalities of people around the world. Once Americans open our mouths to speak, our accent is a dead giveaway. We learned from ladies at church that Paula's hair styles, makeup, clothing, attire, glasses and even posture provided unsubtle clues as to our nationality. So much for blending in!

Family and Friends Welcome

We were delighted to host one hundred nine visitors while we lived in the U.K., not even counting repeat visitors that came to stay with us on multiple occasions. Our visitors included my Mother, Paula's parents, brothers and sisters from both sides of the family, many uncles, aunts, cousins, nieces, nephews; friends from Chicago, Danville, Brownsburg, Indianapolis, Green Bay, Stockton, Pine Bluff, grade school, high school and college friends, work colleagues from Indianapolis, and even a few surprise guests. Ninety percent of the visitors had to get a passport to come because they'd never before traveled outside of the U.S. The average stay was ten days. My brother, Ben and his wife came every year. I guess they must have really enjoyed London.

Even my old boss from GM came and stayed with us for two weeks. Many other friends came as well. We ran a free bed and breakfast for families, friends or friends of friends to come and stay with us.

Paula became especially adept at making itineraries for our visitors. An itinerary was based on the amount of time they'd be staying. We provided a daily breakfast. But because we worked each day, they were on their own for lunch and we'd either cook dinner or plan a place for everyone to meet up for an evening meal and entertainment, which typically included a visit to the London theatre. Paula's itineraries laid out the key sites to see, tour bus schedules and their routes, restaurants and money exchange rates; the exchange rate was a shock to most visitors. The U.S. dollars didn't go nearly as far in London. During the time we lived there, it cost about one dollar and sixty-five cents to purchase one British pound.

33 Harley House ~ Marylebone Road ~ London, NW1 5HF ~ England
Home Phone 44-171-486-4568 ~ E-mail: SWHITFI664

January 08, 1998

Dear Family and Friends,

We send you greetings from London, England, the land of Afternoon Teas, Christmas Pudding, and a Pub on every corner! As many of you know, 1997 was a year of transition for Paula and I. We were blessed indeed with much change, mostly good but not exclusively. On the not so happy side, we lost our beloved Skippy on March 26th. Skippy was our little Shih Tzu pup. Those of you who knew "Mr. Skip" surely understand how much losing him changed our lives. He became very ill unexpectedly; unfortunately, nothing could be done to save him. And as most of you know, we would have spared no expense! (smile) He was a part of our family for 10 years and we miss him terribly, particularly during the holiday time. It was a tough loss that only a pet lover can truly understand. The love and support that we received from family and so many friends was truly heartwarming. We want to thank each of you for your understanding comfort during that difficult time.

In May, Paula was offered a promotion to be Eli Lilly and Company's General Counsel for its operations in Europe, Middle East and Africa. The only catch was that we would have to move to London, England. We both jumped at the chance; after insuring Sherman's continued employment of course! Paula and I prayed about the opportunity and my employment situation. As most of you know, I essentially had been employed by one company for the past 24 years, General Motors Corporation. Even though the division of the company that I worked for had been sold a few times over the past few years, I had stayed in essentially the same place for quite a while. When Paula was offered the new job we looked into the possibility of me continuing my employment with Rolls Royce (the most recent purchaser of Allison Engine Company). As it turned out, Rolls Royce has a plant site in Bristol, England. I was able to obtain an interview with the Rolls Royce, Bristol Plant site; I interviewed contemporaneously at Lilly. Both interviews went well, and I was blessed to have offers from both companies; an offer of a promotion at Rolls Royce and a very interesting position within the manufacturing organization at Lilly. We learned also, however, that my commuting time to Bristol would have totaled about 4 hours a day. Needless to say, we thought the travel time would get to be a little tiring. Accordingly, I decided to accept the position offered by Lilly. I haven't regretted it for a moment! I feel really challenged and am learning a great deal. God is good; no, he's better than that (smile).

Before moving we had the pleasure of celebrating family reunions with both Paula's side of the family at our home in Brownsburg, Indiana and with my family in Houston, Texas. It was wonderful to get to see everyone before our move and to share the joys and growth of each family member. Paula also had her 40th birthday in August, we celebrated her big milestone in style. She insisted on banners indicating that she was "Simply Fabulous At Forty"; we reluctantly obliged. We had a house full of family and friends from virtually each stage of her life; it was a lot of fun for all concerned.

In August we completed the task of selling our house and cars (with the exception of the Corvette of course, never!). Our belongings were either given away, stored, sold or prepared for shipment. We had several Going Away Parties given for us by wonderful and unforgettable friends from each area of our lives. Our family, friends from work and church hosted venues for our good-byes.   We got to see many of you then; it was a truly moving experience to leave much loved family and friends. But, in so doing, we learned and now know how much we truly love and cherish each of you. For this reason, we know that God certainly has had his hand on our steps and is intimately involved in the changes in our lives. This belief is confirmed for us on a frequent basis. We also know that each of you is only a phone call away, a fact that our telephone bill confirms on a monthly basis (smile)!

Paula has had the chance to travel a lot in her new job. She's been to Germany, Italy, France, Holland, Denmark, Sweden, Switzerland, Belgium, and Spain just to name a few. I get to travel to Basingstoke, England to work, not quite the same, but fun in any event. We have both enjoyed getting to know and learn many new people and cultures.

My brother Ben, his wife Linda (from Pine Bluff, Arkansas) and Paula's cousin André (from Rome, Italy) visited us at Thanksgiving. We had a lovely visit. It was so good to have family with us for the holiday. Surprising as it may seem, England does not celebrate Thanksgiving. They have advised us that they celebrate their day of Thanks on the 4th of July; clear evidence that they are glad to be rid of their unruly coloniers! (smile) We had a little trouble getting a turkey. In fact, the one we purchased had to be rid of its feathers! Oh well, we live and learn. Paula was relieved that Linda was here to deal with the turkey; she claims she wouldn't have known what to do otherwise.

Sherman Louis (my son from Dallas, Texas who is now 18 years old, if you can believe it!) was with us from December 21st through the morning of the 27th to help us celebrate Christmas. Paula and I left London late on the 27th for Strasbourg, France for a weeks holiday. We spent time visiting Strasbourg and the charming little villages around it. We also visited portions of the Black Forrest in Germany, (Freiburg & Offenburg, Germany) about an hours drive from the Alsace Region of France, and Basal, Switzerland. We had a wonderful time and a much needed time of relaxation.

We have joined a church and a fellowship group here in London. Our Church is in short walking distance from our home. Paula and I believe the congregation to be a picture of heaven; virtually every nationality is represented in its numbers. We feel very much at home and are being spiritually fed at All Souls Church. We also have been so blessed with the new friends that we have come to know during our brief tenure here.

All in all, we love our new lives, new city and new home (technically referred to as a "Flat" in Londonese). We pray that you are all well and that your holidays and New Year are blessed and filled with joy. Please keep us in your prayers. Also, keep us on your list of places to visit.   We have four bedrooms; quite spacious by London standards. May you be blessed with plenty of God's goodness in '98. We love and miss you all.

Merry Christmas & God Bless,

Sherman
and
Paula

THE WHITFIELDS OF LONDON

Dear Family & Friends,

As we come to the close of another year, our thoughts turn to our family and our many friends, both old and new. We want to wish each of you a very blessed Christmas and a wonderful beginning to the new Millennium.   It has been an outstanding year. We continue to love living in and learning more about England. We thought we would give you an update on how we've been keeping ourselves busy this past year.

The Whitfield's Year In Review

Spiritual Life

We continue to be blessed by our membership in All Souls Church. It is truly a multinational congregation populated with people from all over the world. Indeed, it is a picture of heaven in terms of having people from every nation and language. We attend a wonderful bible and prayer fellowship group hosted bi-weekly at the home our dear friends James and Marion Barrett. Sherman also co-leads a prayer and bible study group at work. The group meets each Friday at lunch time.

Work Life

Paula's continues to love her work. She is General Counsel of European Operations at Lilly. She travels about fifty percent of the time and is responsible for the 15 European Member State countries, plus Norway and Switzerland. Because Sherman is "low maintenance" (smile), her traveling is no problem. We live within walking distance of Paula's office; Sherman's office is about a one hour's drive from London at the Lilly's UK Affiliate located in Basingstoke. (It's clear that Paula is the one that found the Apartment (known as a "Flat" in Londonese) on the final house hunting trip (smile)). Sherman is responsible for purchasing all raw materials and actives ingredients for the site. The site manufactures product for Lilly's global operations; he also has auditing responsibilities for suppliers of the UK site. Sherman's role involves travel within the UK and to Germany, France, and Spain. He also truly enjoys his work, particularly the opportunity it provides him to work with his local English colleagues.

Social Life

The year started with a vacation to Northern Africa (Marrakech, Morocco) for a week. We took a balloon ride over the Sahara Desert, visited the Atlas Mountains, toured the city center and country side. We also managed to purchase a beautiful hand woven rug that *reportedly* took two ladies a year to make by hand. Sherman was pictured and named in the Basingstoke newspaper for his work in raising money for the earthquake victims in Turkey. Paula was invited and attended a session of the English Houses of Parliament. We also were honored to have lunch with her Majesty the Queen (along with about 500 others!) It was hosted by the American Ambassador to England. Sherman was able to join Paula in Sweden, Denmark, Holland, Greece, Spain, France, and Belgium. We have averaged one visit a month to the Theatre to see either a Musical or a Play.   We cook less than once a week, which means we eat out quite a bit; those of you that know us well can appreciate that is nothing new! But why wouldn't we with the choice of Indian, Thai, French, Italian, Chinese, Japanese, Greek, Turkish, Afgan foods, to name a few. English food was not mentioned because nobody eats English food, if they can help it. (smile) We also have spent a number of weekends visiting the old English countryside. When we say old, we mean old. For example, we stayed in a Bed and Breakfast that was built in 1500; but places like this are common over here. We visited the U.S. for Paula's Family Reunion in July and in August for Sherman's Family Reunion in Atlanta, Georgia. Paula also got to visit her brother Steve, his wife Christine and Nik & Tallie on this visit home. It was wonderful to see everyone. In September we headed to the South of France & Northern Italy for a two week Holiday. We visited San Tropez, Cannes, Nice, Monaco, and San Remo.

<u>London Visitors & Travel</u>

We were delighted to open our home to family and friends this year. The first visitors in '99 were our good friends Johnnie and Amre Carey from Danville IL.. They spent a week enjoying the sights and sounds of London. Next came Sherman's favorite Uncle Hules (aka Buck) and Aunt Ola Dale from Chicago IL. We were happy to have Paula' cousin Andre and his friend Sharyn spend some time with us as well. Next were Paula and Sherman's friend Alecia DeCoudreaux from Indianapolis and her mother Viola and Aunt Nita from Cape Cod. Next to arrive and take London by storm were Bill and Judy Denhart, dear friends from Brownsburg, IN. Paula's Sorority Sister Yvette Johnson Estelle, a flight attendant for American also came through a few times. Next, Mary Martin, Paula's life long family friend from Chicago, IL. visited for a few days on her way to Paris. In mid-November Paula visited the U.S. She was delighted to visit her brother Bruce, his wife Kelly and children Brittany, Leslie and Nicole in California, she then visited family and friends in Indianapolis and Chicago. At Thanksgiving Sherman's brother Ben arrived from Pine Bluff, Ark. making his annual pilgrimage to London to share Thanksgiving dinner with his brother and sister-in-law. December will bring Sherman Louis from Dallas, Texas and Paula's youngest brother Jeffrey and his wife Donna from Bloomington, Ill. for the Christmas holiday. We can hardly wait for the time to enjoy our family and for the time off to celebrate Christmas and the New Year in style .

We pray that you are all well and that your holidays and New Year are blessed and filled with love, joy and peace. Please keep us in your prayers. Also, keep us on your list of places to visit. Having family and friends visit us helps to make London feel more and more like home. May you be blessed with plenty of God's goodness in 2000. We love and miss you all.

Love You Always,

Sherman & Paula

P.S. Our addresses are as follows: Sherman & Paula Whitfield
            33 Harley House
            Marylebone Road
            London, England NW1 5HF
            Telephone: 44-171-486-4568 (for dialing from the U.S. first dial 011)
  Sherman's E-Mail: SWHITFI664@AOL.com
   Paula's E-Mail: PAULATWHIT@AOL.com

Journey to Success Notes:

CHAPTER THIRTEEN

RETURNING TO LILLY CORPORATE HEADQUARTERS

After five years working and living in England, Paula was informed that we would be repatriated to the United States. She wasn't changing jobs; she simply was being asked to do her job from Corporate Headquarters. We weren't happy about the prospect. Her job was challenging enough already and required significant travel. But, traveling to Europe and places closer by from England was one thing; doing it from the U.S. was another thing altogether. Paula's repatriation meant I was in for a job change as well. Since our work visas were driven by Paula's position, I was unable to work in the U.K. once she left. While far from delighted with this news, we'd known this day would come. We understood how blessed we were to have had the opportunity to live abroad for five years. When we accepted the assignment, we'd been told that we would be there for between three to five years. But most people got to stay for less than three years. Because Lilly had lost the patent suit involving its blockbuster antidepressant Prozac, the company was tightening its belt in many ways. We were just one family caught in the proverbial crosshairs. Given sixty days to make the move back home, we started the transition process.

My first order of business was to find a job back at Lilly in Indianapolis. Keep in mind, I had never worked for Lilly before our move. So, for me, it was just like my move to London. I knew very few Lilly people and very few knew me. However, because of Paula's astute negotiations when I'd been hired, I was already a U.S. employee and, thus, presumably entitled to a position at Corporate. But, finding the *right* position was the key. The folks in the Indianapolis Human Resources department made a few calls to Basingstoke to determine where my skills would fit best. The most common response they heard was that I was a natural "people person." My uppermost input was that I preferred an individual contributor role verses one where I would have to manage people. I'd learned in my times at Allison, Rolls Royce and at Lilly, that I favored positions where I'd be judged on my individual performance as opposed to on my management of the performance of others. After several interviews, the same Lilly Vice President that had spoken up for me when I'd been hired stepped up to the plate again. Bill Smith, aka "Smitty," offered me a job in the Office of Alliance Management.

Repatriation

We were moving back to Corporate and Lilly was committed to finding a job for me on our return. In some ways, we were looking forward to returning home. We knew that this day would come. Building equity in a home of our own was necessary if we were to meet our long-time goal of owning it out right before we retired. And, being geographically closer to family and our friends definitely had its advantages. But, we were not anticipating it enthusiastically. I knew that the infinitesimal second we landed, I would become not an American but a *male black* American. I would be treated, as all black Americans are treated, with less respect, less appreciation of my skills and less acknowledgement of my humanity. While I knew I had plenty of "privileges," the one I was *not* blessed with at birth was white privilege. Again, imbued with all of the stereotypes white society has put on black people, my outwardly perceived worth would be diminished. Not my self-worth though; that can be lessened only if one allows it.

Our return involved many of the same steps we took when leaving. While in the U.K., we'd bought lots of stuff e.g., furniture, electronics, fans, (remember, there's no air conditioning in most homes in the U.K.) lamps, television sets and many other light household items. Again, we went through the keep, sell, giveaway, or toss process. Most of the electrical items we'd purchased wouldn't function in the U.S. without a transformer due to the difference in voltage. So, we sold most of them. We did keep a Bosch refrigerator though. It had a unique design and was shaped differently than the models we saw in the U.S. While we knew its functional life would be decreased running on a transformer, we decided to bring it home anyway for the sake of novelty. We closed out checking and savings accounts, canceled credit cards, notified utility companies, terminated car leases, shut off the cable television and discontinued our discounted international telephone contract. Our most important "to do" on the long list of tasks of repatriating was finding a house to move back to as we'd sold our home in Brownsburg before moving to London.

One of Paula's close friends and legal work colleagues was married to a realtor. Paula and Lu Carole had worked together at Barnes & Thornburg and both ended up joining the Lilly Law Division. So, we'd known Lu Carole and Rob West for years, and they knew our tastes. The advent of shopping for homes via the internet had really taken off since our last home purchase. Rob sent us loads of choices that fit our established criteria via the internet. This helped, somewhat, in narrowing our search. But not much. We thought we knew what we wanted in terms of home size and amenities but were pretty agnostic about location. Because we didn't have kids to enroll, we weren't especially concerned about schools; so, we were left with almost too many choices. Indianapolis and its surrounding area had plenty of homes to choose from; our biggest problem was narrowing it down.

Lilly provided one house-hunting trip. We scheduled a week for the search and had over one hundred potential homes on the list to choose from. First, we looked in Brownsburg. We still had plenty of friends there, and Calvary United Methodist was there and thriving. The town had changed in the five years we'd been gone and in the ten years since we'd initially moved there. The town's diversity had grown significantly in our time away, and we could see many benefits in returning. We saw one house that we put on the "potential" list, but the house-hunting had just begun.

We looked in Brownsburg, Indianapolis, Carmel, Fishers, Noblesville, the Geist area and even Danville (Indiana). But, Paula loved a house in Zionsville when she first laid eyes on it. It had more space than we needed, over eight thousand square feet, but it met every other item on our "want" list e.g., main floor master bedroom, five bedrooms, six bathrooms, a large eat-in kitchen with adjoining hearth room, three fireplaces, a screened porch, adjoining deck and an over-sized wooded lot with loads of privacy. It even had things we didn't know we wanted like two separate his and her bathrooms in the master suite. It had strong possibilities, but I was lukewarm. It wasn't the house that concerned me. My concern was that the house was in a subdivision inhabited by so many Lilly employees. I was ambivalent. Being with Lilly people each and every workday only to come home and be with them again in our free time was my issue. It may come as a surprise to some, but I'm what one would call an extroverted introvert. Translation, I need private time to recharge. So, we kept looking. We looked and looked. We'd find something that met some of the criteria, and Paula would suggest we go back to the Zionsville house to make a comparison. We'd look some more and end up back in Zionsville to take one more look. After at least three trips back to the house, a light finally went off in my head. Maybe this is the house she wants no matter how many houses we see. So, I said, "I think I really like the Zionsville house, what about you?" She laughed. Rob, our friend and realtor, said he and Paula were wondering how long it was going to take for me to figure that out. We made an offer on the house. After a bit of negotiation, it was ours. The home was located in Austin Oaks, a relatively new, well positioned sub-division in Zionsville. While we didn't need good schools, Zionsville was known to have one of the best school systems in the State which always bodes well for home resale values. Though the town wasn't known for its ethnic diversity, it has grown throughout the years since we arrived. It still has a way to go. We were fortunate, however, to have really friendly neighbors that made us feel welcomed from the start. On our flight back to the U.K., I experienced a palatable sense of sadness. I reflected on the many wonderful friends that we had made, the unforgettable places that we'd visited and the many memories we'd made. Blessed beyond measure, we understood that we would be leaving far more behind on departure than we could have ever dreamed.

Word of our imminent departure spread quickly. Formal and informal farewell celebrations were planned at work, our church fellowship group and by other friends we'd made in our time there. My Basingstoke boss hosted a lunch for everyone in the department. At the appointed time, he asked if anyone wanted to make remarks. Every person in attendance spoke about his/her personal relationship with me and how I had impacted their lives. I was more than touched. I hadn't expected such an outpouring of appreciation from my British colleagues. Brits aren't especially well known for public displays of affection. Even more surprising were the remarks made by Phil Cooke, my boss. He reflected on my work and the contributions I'd made while there, but his focus was on how he saw me living out my Christianity both in my work and my daily walk. He said that he'd witnessed my faith in action. He went further to say that my faith had made more of an impact on people that I would never know.

I was shocked. Phil hadn't acknowledged my Christianity before. He'd never attended a bible study. I'd not even sensed he thought about me much, apart from being one of his direct reports. His comments were pointed, specific and sincere. It was a classic case of someone watching and judging one's actions versus listening to the rhetoric one spouts to determine truth. I took his sentiments to heart. The Bible Study team took me out for lunch and included others that I'd interacted with from manufacturing. Other functional areas that I'd worked with in my five years on site stopped by to wish me well. Even the plant manager and many on his staff stopped by to thank me for the spirit and the enthusiasm that I had brought to the site. Never in my work career had I received so much recognition. I was full of gratitude and my self-esteem was at an all-time high. But, I learned a superb lesson too; the power of the word "thank you." It inspires one to want to do more. A simple thank you prompts a welcoming and savoring emotion that can spark joy. I learned to try to do that whenever and wherever I could because it helps others to be at their best.

Paula had many farewell celebrations in her honor as well, but hers were a little different. She was moving back home, but she wasn't changing jobs. Her move was a simple cost-savings maneuver. We weren't happy about it as it would mean more and longer haul travel for Paula as she would continue to have the same job responsibilities. She'd just have to handle the job from Indianapolis. As it turned out, she would maintain her General Counsel position for three more years, a total of eight. The company rewarded her with a promotion to Vice President and Deputy General Counsel at the end of that tenure.

Making My Own Way ~ And Giving Back

The Office of Alliance Management was a new area in Lilly. It was established because following the loss of the Prozac patent, Lilly was seeking new revenue streams. While this had always been something Lilly engaged in, it was now doing so with a- vengeance. While it was understood that Lilly's Research Laboratories had in the past held its own and steadily produced medicines fueled by its own pipeline, experience had taught the leadership that innovation originated in many places. To fill the gap in Lilly's pharmaceutical development pipeline, it was determined that Lilly needed to look both internally and externally. The Office of Alliance Management was established to help manage the relationships between Lilly and the companies it partnered with to bring more innovation more quickly to the market. Sometimes Lilly would partner with a smaller company that had a compound at an earlier phase of development. Lilly would bring its clinical development expertise to the table to facilitate a more expedient move through the regulatory process. Other times, Lilly would need the expertise of another company to assist in the development of a delivery device or to assist in the manufacturing of a given drug. The objective of the newly established office was to make sure that the alliances Lilly contracted for worked, and that both parties got what they'd bargained for. I was assigned to the team that managed manufacturing alliances. In my first assignment, I was given responsibility for nine manufacturing alliances.

At its essence, my job was to:

1. Develop a mission and vision for the partnership.
2. Develop a clear strategic direction, measurable goals and definitive objectives for each partnership.
3. Develop common goals for each partnership clarifying what each party wanted to accomplish, being as specific as possible.
4. Develop metrics for the partnership.

As an Alliance Manager, I'd lead each meeting where the Mission, Vision, Strategic Direction, Goals, Objectives and Metrics were established and monitored the team's progress. On a quarterly basis, I led the meetings where the metrics of the partnership were reviewed to make transparent how each party was living up to its commitments. It was crucial that both parties shared the level of commitment evidenced by their participation in developing the work product outlined above. While each partner had differing responsibilities, it was key that they understood how the work they did helped achieve the overall goals of the alliance.

This job description fit me to a tee. It aligned with the role I had perfected working with my suppliers in Europe. My job was to be a problem-solver, to work on solutions with our suppliers and partners, to engender win-win solutions for both parties and to promote the overall success of the venture for all concerned. The job was right up my alley. I not only had a "place to go," I had a great place to land and one that fit me. I knew this was not a given. I thanked God for giving me a smart wife who saw this coming five years earlier when I was first hired.

It was a year into my new role that I began conducting partnership/alliance management training with my alliance partners so that they clearly understood the process that that I was using to manage our relationship. I gained the reputation of being a superb relationship-builder, communicator and trainer. There was an alliance management certification course offered by a worldwide organization. I signed up to be tested for certification. I sat for the exam and passed it on the first try. Now a certified alliance professional, I was asked to not only manage my nine alliance partners, but to take on the job of being the world-wide collaboration trainer for Achieving Value through Partnership. This was Lilly's proprietary strategic collaboration management training program.

I led training in Japan, China, England, Brazil, Germany, France and Italy. Having traveled to most of these countries while living abroad, I was comfortable with the travel and interaction with the people from these countries. My job satisfaction was off the charts. I enjoyed it as much as I had any job in my career. After two years back in Indianapolis in my Alliance Management role, I received another promotion. Because my alliances were important to the Company, I had become well known, both by my departmental colleagues and by many in senior leadership. Mentoring young talent was something I found refreshing and enjoyable, so I had taken on doing that with a number of employees. Most, but not all of them, were African American. I had a keen desire to share what I had learned of the Lilly system and throughout my life as well. When initiating conversations, I had a few basic questions that I would ask of them:

1. Where do you want to be in five years?
2. How do you plan to get there?
3. How can I help you to achieve your goals?

In my discussions, however, a common and disturbing theme emerged. It was what I came to refer to as the "December Surprise." Countless times, mentees told me of how at each quarterly performance review they'd be told things were going fine. On final review, however, it was a different story. A detailed dissertation of what had *not* been accomplished would be laid bare. For many, this meant either no raise, or a very small one, and the chance for a promotion was never a part of the discussion. Even when this wasn't the experience, others spoke of how they were not given the "tough" or "higher profile" assignments. So, in the end when comparative contributions were discussed in closed-door sessions for purposes of raises, bonuses or promotions, many came up short. The story, while not surprising, was distressing. So, many people that held so much promise were not being developed to be the very best that they could be.

Blame for the December Surprise phenomenon could be explained, at least in part, by the *"nice," "non-confrontational"* culture of Lilly. In my experience, one had to *really* listen closely if you wanted to hear something negative. Pointing out an employee's deficiency wasn't easy for those brought up in Lilly's culture. But, at the end of the year when management had to rate an employee, and do so in comparison to others, the hammer was forced to come down. Management was held accountable for the salary budget being met (and not exceeded), and limitations were in place for the percentage of promotions that would be given each year. The old adage of "that which is measured is focused upon" held true. And, this would come as a total surprise to the novice employee who had been told all year that they were doing fine. Perhaps subtle clues had been given; but for those not knowing what to listen for, the message never came through.

I shared with my mentees how I overcame the December surprise. I would explain that directness and forced clarity was required. At each periodic review with my boss, I would ask several questions:

1. If you were rating me today what rating would I receive?
2. What would you like to see me accomplish this year to feel comfortable with giving me an Exemplary rating?
3. What would you recommend I *stop* doing this year to feel comfortable with giving me an Exemplary rating?

Documentation of the conversation was key. A supervisor worth his or her salt would welcome the discussion. Indeed, if they were doing their jobs they would initiate it, make sure this type of a conversation occurred to get the most out of each employee and to provide for routine coaching opportunities. This is a tried and true way to prevent the December Surprise. While it isn't a guarantee of an exemplary assessment of one's contributions, the discussion forces open, more honest and clearer objective setting. By doing so, one is far less likely to receive an unexpected message at the end of the year. And, in my experience, that leads to improved outcomes and fewer surprises all around.

Meeting An Unmet Need At Lilly

By the end of my tenure at Lilly, I was a mentor to many. Colleagues of many ethnicities, African Americans, whites, Africans, Asians and Latinos approached me for insight and I was happy to provide my perspective. In 2011, Lilly announced its intention to reduce the workforce by a minimum of five thousand employees. This announcement caused significant mental and emotional consternation. In the

135th year history of the company, no one could remember Lilly officially announcing such a reduction in force.

Lilly had always been known as a caring, people-focused company. It often had been said that when you joined Lilly, you joined for life. If one left the company, it was voluntarily or, rarely, (and this wasn't publicized) for poor job performance. When we joined the company, we were told of how Lilly had never once had a layoff. There are stories of how "the Lillys" kept scientists and everyone employed during wars and the Great Depression, even if workers had to sweep floors or paint walls to maintain their employment. So, when it was announced that five thousand jobs were going to disappear, it was a true seismic shock to the Lilly eco-system. Even in making this announcement, however, Lilly showed a real sense of caring and concern for its employees. The leadership would utilize a two-year timeframe to reach the targeted five thousand employees. This did not make employees feel much better, because it was not announced which employees would be laid off or on what schedule. Everyone felt exposed; that the next one laid off could be them. I felt the concern personally, but I also got to hear the vexation time and time again as I mentored younger people. They worried the decision of "last-in-first-out" could be the implemented practice. Many were anxious and wondered whether seniority would trump expertise and how much notice they'd be given before being put out on the street.

My message was simple:

"I understand your concerns but let me give you my perspective. I worked for General Motors for nearly twenty-four years. When GM was planning a layoff, there first would be a rumor of a layoff, not an official announcement providing a two-year notice. And, within two weeks of the "rumor," you were gone! Lilly has given all of us a two-year notice. This gives each of us an opportunity to make ourselves so valuable to the company that we will not be let go. But,

it also provides us time to prepare ourselves for the day that we might be let go."

My message was pointed: Don't allow yourself to be a victim.

This message was so well received by mentees that I decided to share it with the entire company. I took it upon myself, with my own financial resources, to give monthly motivational speeches in venues open to all employees at the Lilly Corporate Center, Lilly Technology Center North and South, and at Elanco. I coined the sessions as "The Empowerment Series."

The attendees included all levels of Lilly employees in all functions of the company, including senior management. I had folks from marketing, sales, finance, legal, human resources, medical, regulatory, quality, safety and all functions within those division, e.g., administrative assistants and even people working on the manufacturing lines making product. Posters were displayed across all sites announcing the dates and times for the events. I'd provide refreshments such as fruit, pastries, coffee, assorted juices and water. I hosted over thirty speaking events encouraging and motivating employees to give Lilly their best work and to prepare themselves for the future to come, whatever that future might be.

My topics were all positive:

- Give It Your Best and Don't Worry About the Rest
- There is Greatness in You
- Your Attitude will Determine Your Altitude
- Top Ten Reasons to be Thankful
- Take This Life and Love It

When I had my performance review, my boss asked me who in Human Resources was sponsoring my Empowerment Series. He said that he had attended some of my talks and thought they were both positive and helpful. He was very impressed. He wanted to give feedback to Human Resources and to include it as an accomplishment in my annual performance review.

I told him no one in Human Resources was sponsoring my series and that I'd decided on my own to do it. I explained how my idea had been sparked by those I was mentoring and my conversations with many other employees. My goal was to try to help relieve some of the stress being experienced by my fellow employees and to do something positive for the company. I explained that in my opinion, it is sometimes best to ask for forgiveness as opposed to permission when you are trying to do something you know is needed. Corporate red tape can hold up progress. He told me to keep doing what I was doing. He very much supported my efforts and said that he would make sure HR did as well.

In truth, everyone thought I had been approved and sponsored to put on the Empowerment Series. I did what I thought was needed. Lilly had been good to me and to my wife, and I felt it was something I could pay forward.

Confidence In Self

Self-confidence is key to becoming the best you can be. It is a special elixir that God places in each of us to help us face the unsurmountable. Confidence in one's self is a special blend of optimism, attitude, experience, knowledge, hope and wisdom. If we are fortunate enough to grow up in a loving and supportive home where self-esteem is encouraged, we gain self-confidence naturally and early. If we are not so fortunate, we need to seek it out in other ways. My advice is to surround yourself with positive people, read positive and uplifting books, learn and practice speaking positively about yourself and do the same for others.

There is an old proverb that says the blood of the covenant is thicker than the blood of the womb. What does that mean? To me that means - yes, DNA matters; yes, the environment in which one is raised matters, but, God's promise is most important of all. He says *we* matter. We *all* matter. He sent his Son to die for us. And, with that new covenant he implanted Greatness within each of us. He loved us before we loved ourselves. And, if he loves us, how can we not take care to love ourselves and others as well.

My sense of optimism is grounded in God's Word. And, through Him I know that I can do all things. I believe firmly that if you *think* you can't do something, you're right; you can't. But, if you *think* you can, you can. Today, decide you can do anything! You can. I have every confidence that you can.

The End

Jeremiah 29:11

"For I know the plans I have for you, declares the Lord, plans for good and not for evil, to give you hope and a future."

Invite Sherman to Inspire and Ignite Your Team!

Presentations by Sherman L. Whitfield:

<u>**How To Be Your Best Series:**</u>

- ❖ Recognize Your Positive Characteristics.
- ❖ Challenge Yourself to be Your Best.
- ❖ Seek Out Positive Mentors and Role Models.
- ❖ Expect Setbacks But Not Turn Backs.
- ❖ Be Responsible - Live by Moral and Ethical Principles.
- ❖ Be Healthy - Be Physically Fit.
- ❖ Be Involved - Serve Your Community.
- ❖ Be Studious – Never Stop Learning.
- ❖ Be Ambitious - Set and Achieve Your Goals.
- ❖ Always Think Positive!

<u>Your Best Days Are Ahead of You Series:</u>

- ❖ Stand Up on the Inside (until you can stand up on the outside).
- ❖ Don't Accept a Bad Situation as a Permanent Situation.
- ❖ You May be Down Now, But…
- ❖ Expect Good Things to Happen to You.
- ❖ Expect to be at the Right Place at the Right Time.
- ❖ Expect Good Favor.

<u>**You Can Make Your Legacy One to Celebrate Series:**</u>

- ❖ Leave a Positive Legacy.
- ❖ Leave a Helping Legacy.
- ❖ Leave a Never Give Up on Life Legacy.
- ❖ Leave a Life of Integrity Legacy.
- ❖ Leave a Can-Do Attitude Legacy.
- ❖ Leave a Love of Family, Friend and Fellowship Legacy.

<u>Your Attitude Will Determine Your Altitude Series:</u>

- ❖ Choose the Right Attitude Today.
- ❖ Choose the Right Attitude Today to Succeed (With your family, your friends, your health, and your work).
- ❖ Choose the Right Attitude to Succeed in Everything.
- ❖ Success *starts* with the Right Attitude.
- ❖ The Right Attitude Does Not Sweat the Small Stuff.
- ❖ Your Level of Success *is* Based on Your Attitude.

Top Ten Reasons To Be Thankful Series:

- ❖ Be thankful for the ones who love you.
- ❖ Be thankful for the job that you have today.
- ❖ Be thankful for your Relationships (good and bad).
- ❖ Be thankful for your health.
- ❖ Be thankful for your ability to help people.
- ❖ Be thankful for the happiness that you have.
- ❖ Be thankful for everything you have accomplished.
- ❖ Be thankful for every second of life that you have.
- ❖ Be thankful for your faith.
- ❖ Be thankful for your family.

Who Sherman Is Today

Sherman believes that every person has greatness inside of them. He believes that everyone has the necessary gifts and abilities to make an authentic impact on the world. His personal story is one that reads like a script written in Hollywood. He was born in Arkansas, one of six children with no father in the home. At a young age, Sherman had to stay out of school to pick cotton to help support his family. Because of this, he failed two grades before he reached junior high school. He had a childhood accident, but, because his family was poor, he wasn't taken to the doctor for treatment. He lost vision in his right eye.

Later in life, Sherman developed prostate cancer. When he received the news, he was on his way to play a round of golf. He told his doctor that he would get back with him after he finished eighteen holes. The next day, he and his wife Paula met with the doctor, listened to the available options and developed an aggressive treatment plan. He has successfully completed the surgery and is continuing the healing process.

When members of his church heard the news of his cancer diagnosis, some were distraught. Sherman attended a prayer meeting and he told the church he wasn't worried. He explained that while he had faith and hoped that he'd recover, he knew that if he didn't he'd spend eternity with Jesus. Again, this reflects Sherman's positive attitude and strong faith.

The most pivotal point of his life was when his father left the family home. His mother and father separated. But, they took their marriage vows seriously, at least the part that said they would stay married until death. They never divorced. After a separation of over fifty-five years, his father became ill and returned home. Sherman's parents spent the last ten years of his father's life as husband and wife. Benjamin Franklin

Whitfield, Sr. died at the ripe old age of 100, a mere four months before his 101st birthday.

Sherman learned at an early age from a severely visually impaired man, Mr. Gooseberry, that in life there would always be trials and tribulations and that only the strong would succeed. Success is an internal construct and a voluntary intentional mindset. One can have all of the mentors, counselors and opportunities to succeed in life, but unless one's heart and mind is focused on success, success will be illusive and never achieved. The opposite is also true. Adversity and harsh circumstances need not define one's life. The challenges one faces are irrelevant, if you choose to deem them so. If one has the internal heart, mindset and the drive to succeed, success will find you. For as the old saying goes; As a man thinks, so is he.

One need only research the lives and experiences of our enslaved ancestors who lived under the most adverse circumstances to see this truth. By perseverance and sheer will, they became some of the world's leading doctors, lawyers, inventors, civil rights leaders and politicians. A few examples include Sojourner Truth (1797-1883), Dred Scott (1799-1858), John Brown (1800-1859), William Harvey Carney (1840-1908), Frederick Douglass (1818-1895), Nat Turner (1800-1831), Sam Sharpe (1801-1832), Olaudah Equiano (1745-1797), Ignatius Sancho (1729-1780), Booker T. Washington (1856-1915), Harriet Tubman (born into slavery in Maryland — died 1913), Lewis Howard Latimer (1848-1928), George Washington Carver (1864-1943), Sarah Breedlove known as Madam C.J. Walker (1867-1919), just to name a few. African Americans emerged from some of the resilient people on earth; our genealogy is strong. That we have survived despite the adversity we've endured is living testament to that strength.

Sherman is convinced that success is an "inside" job. It starts with one believing that God has equipped every person with an intrinsic gift to make a difference in this world. It was this *inside* belief that drove his success with the help of all of those that surrounded him on his journey. As a reference in point, go back to Mr. Gooseberry. He was physically blind but had 20-20 vision with his "can do and never give up attitude." Sherman suffered through poverty, physical hunger, abandonment, racial discrimination, childhood accidents, divorce and cancer; but he has never given up.

His advice to everyone that reads this book is to look inside of yourself and ask the question:

If you think that you can be successful, you are right. If you think you can't be successful, you are right as well. It is truly up to you. The self-teaching and ruminations in your mind will be your self-fulfilling prophecy. "For as a man thinketh in his heart, so is he." Proverbs 23:7

Despite all of the challenges Sherman experienced, like many people before him, he never gave up. At a young age, he had the audacity to see obstacles as opportunities. Sherman graduated valedictorian of his high school class. He went on to work his way through college and graduated with honors from the University of Arkansas and later got his

Master's Degree from Indiana Wesleyan University, again with honors.

Sherman continued his learning and development as he successfully navigated the ranks of General Motors, Rolls Royce, and later Eli Lilly and Company. Prior to starting his own company, Sherman used his motivational speaking skills at corporations like Catalent Pharmaceuticals, Patheon Pharmaceuticals, WellPoint, St. Vincent's Hospital, the United Way and many others.

Today, as a motivational speaker, entrepreneur and owner of The Whitfield Motivational Speaking, LLC, Sherman's high-energy motivational keynote programs have positioned him to becoming one of the fastest growing speakers on the market. Sherman is driven by a mission to impact and inspire others to believe, "There is Greatness Inside of YOU... and YOU really can make a difference in this world using the gifts that God already has given YOU!"

If you are looking for an authentic speaker who will energize, motivate and inspire your organization with a great message about personal responsibility and leadership and will leave your team with practical steps they can take to "Position Themselves for Success," then get ready for Sherman Whitfield. His story alone will inspire you to be the best that you can be, against all odds!

Sherman L. Whitfield is President and CEO of Whitfield Motivational Speaking, LLC. He is a retired Director of Eli Lilly and Company based in Indianapolis, Indiana. He is a graduate of the University of Arkansas, Pine Bluff, with a bachelor's degree in Business Administration. He earned a master's degree in Business Management from Indiana Wesleyan University.

Sherman has spoken in the United States, Europe, Latin America and Asia. He has visited more than thirty countries, including Argentina, Austria, Australia, Belgium, Brazil, Canada, China, Czech Republic, Denmark, England, France, Germany, Hungary, Ireland, Republic of Ireland, Israel, Italy, Japan, Jamaica, Kenya, Mexico, Morocco, the Netherlands, New Zealand, Norway, Poland, Portugal, Scotland, Singapore, South Africa, Spain, Switzerland, Tanzania, Turkey, and Wales, to name a few. Steven Turner wrote about Sherman's life testimony in the book entitled *Amazing Grace*, a book that included others of note like Joan Collins and Bono. Sherman has appeared as a guest on two television shows and has even met the Queen of England. He is married to Paula Taylor Whitfield, the love of his life, is the proud father of Sherman Louis, grandfather of Destiny and Louis, is devoted to his beloved Shih Tzu Sydney and, he is a committed Christian.